Gathering Noise from My Life

DONALD ANDERSON

Gathering Noise from My Life

A Camouflaged Memoir

UNIVERSITY OF IOWA PRESS

IOWA CITY

University of Iowa Press, Iowa City 52242
Copyright © 2012 by Donald Anderson
www.uiowapress.org
Printed in the United States of America

Design by Sara T. Sauers

The University of Iowa Press is a member of Green Press
Initiative and is committed to preserving natural resources.

Printed on acid-free paper

Library of Congress Cataloging-in-Publication Data
Anderson, Donald, 1946 July 9–
Gathering noise from my life: a camouflaged memoir /
Donald Anderson.
 p. cm.
Includes bibliographical references.
ISBN-13: 978-1-60938-111-0, ISBN-10: 1-60938-111-4 (pbk)
1. Anderson, Donald, 1946 July 9– I. Title.
PS3601.N54Z46 2012
813'.6—dc23
[B] 2012002439

FOR

Donald Arthur Anderson (1920–1993)
Zola Maxine Anderson (1925–2009)

Author's Note

I CONCERN MYSELF IN THIS BOOK WITH MATTERS OF WAR, RACE, religion, memory, illness, and family, sources of humor and horror. And: boxing, which has been reported in literature from Homer on. Although a questionable and hardly perfect sport, there are times when individuals in the ring, acknowledging the risk (like writers), nearly grasp perfection. *You can run, but you can't hide* applies to both professions. My gratitude to the writers I quote, reading being the principal—reliable and abiding—pleasure of my life. I trust the enclosed short quotes will entice readers to seek the writers' full texts, which is part of the drive of this book. And this: The cruelest deception would be amnesia, for not to know who you were is to not know who to be. *We are where we've been and what we've read.*

I reiterate here some facts and attitudes and words underscored in previous work—in particular, *Fire Road, When War Becomes Personal,* and *Aftermath.* I am indebted to those publishers as well as to the editors of several journals, most notably, *EPOCH, North American Review, Fiction International, Michigan Quarterly, Connecticut Review, Massachusetts Review,* and *Weber Studies,* who have supported my efforts that contribute to this book. My heart-deep thanks to the University of Iowa Press for backing this, my third book with them, and an especial thanks to Joseph Parsons, my stalwart editor there.

PART

I

We have been through them now, the silver
anniversaries: VE-Day,
the Bomb, the wreck
of Japan, all
misted in quaintness—and still
they keep coming,
brown women swirling past,
the armies somewhere behind them, burning
the villages: always the same,
the same weary women each year,
muddy skeletons lugging
the brass pots, tugging the delicate children,
camping in culverts, eating grass—
and the rich bombers run
on their shabby targets; kids
in helmets inch
through torn jungles; somewhere at sea,
ships lob shells
at the horizon—it is all a memory
of old men:
the brave planes limping home,
balding heroes sending
their sons to glory, the bleeding
always the same, like father
like son, breastplate
and buckler rusting
in a dream of blood we
move through, open-eyed
sons of our dreaming fathers
waiting for all the memories
to fade.

—PHILIP APPLEMAN, *The Persistence of Memory*

Every human being is an archeological site. What passes for roots is actually a matter of sediment, of accretion, of chance and juxtaposition. —LUC SANTE, The Factory of Facts

I can't eat a peach without first skinning it.

My father's father, James Arthur Anderson, owned family land near Moab that he lost in a poker game to a Utah judge. To remedy this loss, he made and sold Prohibition hooch to Jack Mormons. In time, his selling to Utes on the reservation set the Feds on his trail. Loading up Grandmother LeVone, my father and his sister, Ramona, he headed north. When they ran out of gas in Montana, they parked. Butte is where I was born and schooled.

The reliable thing about a road is that its decisions have been made.

Butte, Montana, is the home of Evel Knievel. The Bobby Knievel I knew was a jailbird, penned up for petty crimes and robbery. At the height of his fame, Evel, his own two arms in casts, attacked a book author with a baseball bat. Knievel had been upset with the author's characterizations of the daredevil's announced core values.

Harry "Swede" Dahlberg was my high school gym teacher. Coaching four sports (for more than 40 years), his teams won 26 state championships. In the 1960s, he just taught gym. A child of the nineteenth century, he served in the Navy in the Great War and was an Army PE instructor during World War II. Heading toward 70, Coach Dahlberg performed 50 perfect pushups at the beginning of each gym class, and would converse while he did his pull-ups. "Dry your face before your ass," he advised.

Butte, Montana—"The Richest Hill on Earth"—was once the largest city between St. Louis and Seattle. In 1867, the peak of the placer boom had the city's population at 500. It halved over the next two years. Then, quartz deposits were discovered. Based first on silver, then copper, mining barons became Montana's first millionaires. In 1884, there were 300 operating mines, 4,000 posted mining claims, nine quartz mills, and four smelters, all operating 24/7, making Butte the planet's largest producer of copper. In 1899, Marcus Daly merged with Rockefeller's Standard Oil Company to create the Amalgamated Copper Mining Company. By 1910, having bought up the smaller mining companies, Amalgamated changed its name to the Anaconda Copper Mining Company, the largest corporate power in Montana. Through the 1950s, the company owned every newspaper published in the state, the fourth largest after Alaska, Texas, California.

Butte's Miners' Union formed in 1878, sending the largest delegation to the International Workers of the World's founding convention in Chicago in 1906. Butte became known as the "Gibraltar of Unionism," but worker frustration at the company's deaf ear to demands led to violence in 1914 and 1917, violence involving guns, dynamite, federal troops, and murder. In a singular case, Butte's mayor shot and killed Erick Lantilla, a Finnish miner, after the disgruntled Finn had stabbed the mayor.

In 1917—the city's population at a peak of 100,000—168 men were killed in a mine fire: a fire that remains the worst disaster in U.S. mining annals. A frayed electrical cable being lowered down the main shaft sparked the dry timber lining. With the Great War clamoring for copper, all of Butte's mines were working at capacity, and the Speculator mine had nearly half its 2,000 miners below ground when the fire struck, scattering flames down the shaft and into the drifts and crosscuts. Two years before the Speculator calamity, 16 shift bosses and assistant foremen, who had surfaced for their lunch, stood around the main shaft of the Granite Mountain mine awaiting the 12:30 whistle as the signal to return underground. Also awaiting descent were 12 cases of dynamite. Just as the whistle blew, so did the powder. Fingers, identified by rings, were found a mile distant.

1995. In a more recent explosion, 168 people died at the hand of Timothy McVeigh when he bombed the Alfred P. Murrah Federal Building in Oklahoma City, Oklahoma.

You might not think so, but a deep-shaft mine is not cool and damp like a cavern. It is hot and humid, like Mississippi.

1964. I graduated Butte High and my father, as he'd promised, got me on at the Mountain Con, the mine where he was employed as safety engineer. My first job was assisting a contract miner (experienced humpers paid for the volume of ore they moved) whose regular partner hadn't shown up for work the day after payday. I'd stood that day in the rustling line and was hired for a pre-determined day's pay of $21. I went to work with the miner, mucking out a stope that had been drilled and blasted the shift before.

In a shaft mine, what you might call a tunnel is called a drift. Stopes (pronounced with a long o, like stōve) slant off vertically mined shafts called raises. Stopes follow the ore veins, because shaft mining is about the removal of high-grade ore.

Entr'acte

Our mucking machine, like everyone's, powered by hydraulics, was a scoop—a steel bucket on cables and pulleys rock-bolted into the face of the stope. When the cable snapped, my partner and I dragged it, like road kill, to the tracks where we laid it on one of the ore car steel rails. Here, he meant to trim the frayed ends in order to resplice them. My partner knelt by the rail and arranged the heavy snake. I handed him the axe.

I was asking questions and, in the process of answering me and trimming the cable, the man lopped off his left index finger. It was a powerful swing and a clean cut, just shy of the knuckle, toward the wrist. The man removed his glove to stanch the bloody pump. He didn't shriek when the axe fell or when he observed the result. He wrapped the wound with shirt cloth he'd torn away with one swift move with his good right hand. *Shit*, he murmured, then rose to stand in his half

shirt. He could have been a statue, a bronze man in a helmet, a hero, an actor in a movie starring Victor Mature. The miner's reaction made me think of Ulysses or Samson.

I stooped to retrieve the digit. It was still in its little glove case, like a gift jackknife. We headed for the station, where a massive box constructed of lagging (rough-cut 2×8s) housed coils of pipe through which water flowed for drinking, for drilling, and for quelling dust. Each morning, on each level of the mine (we were on the 5200 level, a mile deep) block ice was shipped down and dumped into these boxes to chill the water.

I had carried the axe, and chopped on a block for ice to fill my hardhat. I dumped the finger from the glove, then covered it with ice.

At the lighted station, we rang for the cage. My father, in his role as safety engineer, arrived with the shift boss. He transferred the finger and ice to his hat. My partner, my father, the shift boss, and the iced bone and flesh were hoisted up. My father congratulated me for thinking of ice. He called me *Donnie* in front of the men.

I reattached the lamp to my hardhat and hoofed it back to the stope and the cable. There were ice chunks caught in the hardhat webbing. I stuck two pieces in my mouth. I ate lunch, then looked at my watch and waited. Temperatures at 5200 feet were generally in the 90s. I was sweating when I saw light approaching. I guessed it was my father coming to check on me, but it was my partner. He had been to St. James Hospital where his finger had been reattached.

My partner walked me through resplicing the snapped cable, and we went back to work with me operating the mucking machine. In the middle of it all, I shot my partner a look. *Didn't want to miss the shift,* he said. He held the ungloved hand in front, as if to know where it was. Its wrapping shone white in our lamplight.—from "Rock Salt"

During the 1960s in Butte, the Chamber of Commerce sponsored a "Clean-up, Paint-up, Fix-up" campaign. The slogan *Butte is my town— and I like it!* was plastered defensively all over the town. In addition to Knievel, Butte produced the now-defunct Berkeley Pit, an expanse that Robert Craig Knievel, even in his greenest youth, would not have attempted to clear. The rising groundwater in this, the nation's deepest

abandoned mined pit, is so poisonous with dissolved metal concentrations that ducks or geese, landing in its inviting mile-deep shining, die. Loudspeakers blare recorded shotgun blasts to discourage the fowl but have not proven convincing. Iridescent carcasses pester the banks.

My first Air Force assignment was in Biloxi, Mississippi. I reported in the summer of 1971, the same year Coach Dahlberg died. Having spent the bulk of my life in the Rocky Mountains I was unprepared for a humidity that proved physical, an objection impossible to refute.

Three heavyweight boxing champions: John L. Sullivan, himself, as well as Jim Jeffries and Bob Fitzsimmons, all fought bouts in Butte. Holding the record for the lowest winter temperature (-61°F) in the contiguous United States, Butte is where J. Edgar Hoover assigned FBI agents who nettled him.

In Biloxi, when the sun went down, it got hotter.

What are we but history with a small *h* in history with a big *H*?

A Mormon bishop warned my grandfather about the Feds.

A person's history is not measured by progress or kings but by seasons and time.

The Berkeley Pit's heavy metal water is rising at a rate of 5,000 gallons per minute, 7.2 million gallons per day. Situated above much of Butte's population, the Berkeley Pit has a current water depth of some 5,200 feet (the same depth the shaft was sunk at the Mountain Con, where I had been employed as a miner). The level at which general flooding will occur is 5,410 feet. The combination of "The Richest Hill on Earth" and the Silver Bow Creek flowing down the Clark Fork drainage has been named the largest Superfund site in U.S. history, covering, as it does, some 100 miles in length. The Clark Fork is no longer the water Meriwether Lewis and William Clark committed to map and drank. It is not water you can bathe in.

That summer in Biloxi, I consumed shrimp and iced beer. That was the summer James Earl Jones regally starred as Jack Johnson in *The Great White Hope*.

At 19, I left Butte to live in France for two and one-half years as a Mormon missionary. Not long after returning, I self-defrocked, sending a letter of disavowal to Salt Lake City requesting excommunication.

As a boy, James Earl Jones suffered from what he has called "incapacitating" stuttering, something you would not know from studying his long stage and film career. Currently, he is heard worldwide intoning *This is . . . CNN.*

I didn't miss Butte when I lived in France. There were too many distractions, not the least of which was the French language itself that rushed at my ears like static. The first time I missed Butte was when the Air Force assigned me to Strategic Air Command Headquarters in Omaha, Nebraska. I'd lived most of my life at the base of the Continental Divide in Montana, where the sun rose from behind and set upon peaks. In Nebraska, the sun didn't know where to be.

James Earl Jones cured his stutter by reciting aloud the King James Bible and Shakespeare's plays.

Faith, like a jackal, feeds among the tombs, and even from these dead doubts she gathers her most vital hope.—Herman Melville

Before I finished college, I held three union cards: Mine Mill Workers, Teamsters, and the International Union of Bricklayers and Allied Craftworkers. I worked in mines and smelters, and in construction, where I carried hod.

In 1978, my father called from Butte to inform me that the Mormon Church would now permit black men to be ordained into the priesthood. To this point, blacks could be baptized (and pay tithes) but their full participation was restricted. In the Mormon hierarchical patriarchy,

blacks had heretofore held no positions of authority, nor had they been allowed into the "sacred" temples.

Originally, *hod* was a three-sided box carried on the shoulder for transporting bricks and mortar to support bricklayers. Today, high scaffolding incorporates elevators and wide-enough planking to allow for wheelbarrows. Hod carrying remains unskilled work.

As of today, blacks are, of a sudden, acceptable?
No, as of June 1st, my father said.
You mean God has caved in the face of the NAACP? I couldn't help myself.
What do you mean?
You telling me the prophet has had a revelation about blacks? Then: *Like Brigham Young did about plural marriage?* Then: *Polygamy was against the law, Dad. Shouldn't we recognize a difference between divine decree and political expediency?*
I thought you'd be happy about the Negroes.
I am . . . now BYU can get some running backs.
I was sorry the minute I said it.

Jack Johnson, the first black heavyweight champion, died the year I was born: 1946. Johnson died in a car wreck in North Carolina, in his 69th year. My two grandfathers died at 69. As did Evel Knievel.

The Church's "revelation" that lifted the ban on blacks, ended NAACP protests and widened the world for proselytizing. The Mormon Church has tripled in size since 1978. Racial exclusivity and polygamy remain, in the Church's public relations' terms, "primary misconceptions" about its people and doctrine.

Jack Johnson was convicted in 1912 of violating the Mann Act for transporting his fiancée across state lines (from Pittsburgh to Chicago) and was sentenced to a year in prison. The woman was white.

The law named after its author, a Republican congressman from Illinois, was officially known as the White Slave Traffic Act. Other

notables prosecuted under its jurisdiction are Charlie Chaplin, Frank Lloyd Wright, and Chuck Berry. Recently, federal prosecutors toyed with charging New York's governor Eliot Spitzer with violation of the Mann Act.

Jack Johnson was married twice, both times to Caucasians.

The highest-paid man on the construction crew was not the senior bricklayer—it was the man who erected the scaffolding, a barrel-shaped human with log arms. He claimed to have bested Merlin Olsen in an arm wrestle. Olsen carried hod for the crew before playing football in college. The construction company was based in Olsen's hometown, Logan, Utah, where Olsen All-Americaned at Utah State.

The first dead person I saw was an Algerian who'd been stabbed in a brawl and lay on the cobblestones, leaking. The Algerians, who stood about, ignored us—a couple of white kids in black suits, gaping. We wore black plastic tags etched in white: *Missionaire Mormone*.

In France, I met a 17-year-old who struck me as the most sophisticated woman I had yet met. She spoke French and smoked cigarettes.

My father clicked his teeth when he clipped his nails. He had strong teeth for a kid raised without milk or a proper diet. He experienced but one cavity over the term of his life, though a back tooth did crack when he was 60. He had a habit of chewing ice. When I was a kid, we had a cow. My jaw is amalgam and crowns.

In 1960, Harold Perkins socked me in the stomach after I said I was happy the Pirates defeated the Yankees in the World Series. My father liked it that Vernon Law, the Pirates' ace pitcher who won two games and started the seventh, was a practicing Mormon who believed walking a batter as sinful as hard drink and tobacco.

Muhammad Ali very much admired James Earl Jones's portrayal of Jack Johnson.

When my father's tooth cracked, he had it pulled but did not replace it.

Pittsburgh: whose professional teams (Pirates, Steelers, Penguins) all parade the same hues. Canary yellow and black.

1932. Six Butte youths are killed by the premature explosion of a number of sticks of dynamite at the Meaderville baseball park, where they were celebrating the Fourth of July. "Swede" Dahlberg had coached nine years already.

Upon retiring from baseball, Vernon Law coached baseball at Provo High, across the street from BYU.

An undergraduate English major, I hoisted my hand at Utah State to ask what was so special about *this Faulkner*. The professor, to his abounding credit, disregarded me.

In the series that the Pirates won on Mazeroski's unexpected homer in the bottom of the ninth in game 7, the new champs had been outscored 55-27 and out-hit 91-60. No wonder Harold Perkins socked me. No wonder my father praised Vernon Law's clean living and Mormon connection. Had he forgotten that it was Clemente who kept Pittsburgh's rally going with a hit in the eighth inning of the final game?

Though a lousy father, undependable husband, and atrocious drunk, has anyone written so angelically as John Cheever?

One of my brighter students compared reading Hemingway to riding in a car with someone learning to drive stick.

Another professor, with a pate and a beard like Shakespeare, taught the Bard. He had assigned me a B on a paper. I stood outside his open door hoping to catch his eye. Finally, he looked up and said, "Yes?" I informed the professor that I'd never received a B on a paper. He, for a moment, went back to his work, then looked up again. "Imagine that," he said.

I can milk a cow. I can string barbed wire. I can safely fell a tree. I can solder.

"Grog" Robinson's name was derived from his capacity to drink, or the fact he was a collegiate rodeo champ, a broncobuster. But he hadn't landed on his head enough to forgo buying a four-bedroom to house six roommates, two to a room. (Grog slept in the single master.) Our rent paid Grog's mortgage. When he sold the house, Grog had lived rent-free and, like the rest of us, had completed college but also had garnered a profit. I've no idea what became of Grog. Have you seen him?

My father told me that when he was young (6 or 7?) he would sweep through fields with his father, tossing sand to discover the glass jars of moonshine that competitors were hiding. As a man, my father understood that his father had been putting the two of them in danger. *On the other hand*, my father defended, *my sister and I were the only kids in Vernal, Utah, wearing shoes. We had shoes*, he said, *so we wore them*.

One of my grown sons informed me that the Subaru is a lesbian car. I disputed his claim as unfounded stereotyping, like saying softball and powerlifting are lesbian sports. *Well?* he asked. Then about the Subarus: *You'll see*. Two weeks later: *Well?*

I'd rather slug a milkshake than a Gin and Tonic. I drink gin every day. A milkshake is an infrequent treat.

Despite his high church standing and his teetotaler belief, my father displayed patience with drunks, as if he saw earnest virtue in their focus.

When I spied the blue Volvo sporting a FREE TIBET bumper sticker, I gagged. Then: Our two cars side-by-side at the stoplight: The man appeared to be Tibetan.

My mother and Queen Elizabeth II were born the same year.

Tall, nonfat, with whip, vanilla latte.

Queen Elizabeth II has reigned since 1952, the year I walked into first grade.

In the barn, where we milked the cow, I sequestered *Police Gazettes* and the lingerie pages from the Sears catalog. The *Police Gazette* contained blurred photos of strippers and whores, and lurid stories about murder and sex. Whence the *Gazettes?* Were they my father's? I do know he kept a pinup calendar in his sock drawer. The pages from Sears, I tore out myself.

In junior high I traced a picture of Jesus and colored it in with pastel chalk. I made Jesus white with brown hair, blue eyeballs. You couldn't see his ears. I sprayed the pastels with a finisher and framed it. My father asked directly if I'd traced the picture or if I'd drawn it. I said I drew it. For a couple of years, my work hung in my parents' bedroom.

My mother was 30 and I 10 when I observed her nude in a tub in Kansas. We'd driven the Ford to visit an aunt and an uncle. The aunt was my mother's sister; the uncle a preacher and founder of a ranch for Christian but forlorn children. Aside from my school's cafeteria, it was the only place I'd ever seen a milk dispenser with a crotch to press your glass against. In a strange, huge house I'd barged into a bathroom. I took a step back. "As you leave, close the door behind," my mother suggested. I peed in the corn while the dog watched.

My grandfather claimed Jack Dempsey fought Jess Willard in 1919 for the heavyweight crown with cracked ribs, and that he, my grandfather as a sparring partner, had cracked them. He also claimed to have witnessed Jack Dempsey bend a horseshoe flat with his hands. And he told me stories of his days in the Yukon when he was just a few years older than I when I was listening. As I heard it from him, my grandfather pretty much walked to and from Alaska.

Who can top Robert Penn Warren's run of poetry during his last 20 years except, maybe, Auden or Marianne Moore. Elizabeth Bishop?

Melanoma.

Jack's given name was William Harrison Dempsey (after the president). His parents were Mormon converts who'd moved from West Virginia to Manassa, Colorado. Dempsey, the "Manassa Mauler," is said to have proclaimed that he wished he were a better Mormon and not the "Jack" Mormon he was (which is one version of the source of the term). Early on, Dempsey fought under the name of "Kid Blackie" in Colorado mining towns within train rides of Manassa.

Founded by Mormon pioneers escaping Illinois, the turquoise-mining town of Manassa consists of one perfect square-mile grid made up of eight blocks by eight blocks. There are two churches in Manassa: the Church of Jesus Christ of Latter-Day Saints and St. Theresa of the Baby Jesus. One street is named Jack.

Instead of working in the mines in Butte, my grandfather, too, would don boxing gloves and battle. Paydays, he would show at a mine at the shift change to challenge all comers. Someone would pass a hat and the winner would walk with the cash. My grandfather made a living this way, or at least what he needed to fuel the cards and the booze.

"Kill the body, the head dies," my grandfather informed me on the day he left our house for the county home. Quoting Joe Louis, he had handed me his boxing gloves. They weren't pillow gloves; they were thin as winter mittens. Mitts on, I felt dangerous. Along the cracks in the gloves ran slivers of a color like rust, as if it were blood and not time that had broken the leather.

I knew a heroin addict in college named Sally who owned a health food store named *Good*. Sally would only drink water-processed decaffeinated coffee.

When my grandfather passed, he'd suffered such fits from alcohol withdrawal and a bleeding gut that his head had curled to touch his knees. Before he himself died, my father told me that they'd had to crack his father's back to shoehorn him into the casket. My father also said that this was what his own father had predicted.

I once lucked into a lunch with Joseph Heller. *Catch-22*, the movie, had just been released. A longtime fan of the novel, I was disappointed with the two-hour take of a book that takes a month to read. I asked Mr. Heller why he'd allowed the movie. *For the money*, he said, as if I had two heads.

I did not buy a hybrid. I bought a full-sized SUV with an engine as efficient as a sumo wrestler's heart.

I can't eat a tomato like an apple, though my father could, if he had salt.

Good cholesterol?

The children I teach in college were born about the same number of years from the Vietnam War as I was born from the First World War.

As if China will do its part to curb petroleum glut and pollution . . .

How to Pen a List:
So what makes a country, apart from tangled history? Baked goods. Churches. Weather. The habit of discretion. Fried potatoes. Shrubbery. The color gray. The elaborate mandarin ritual that attends commercial transactions, or even just step into a shop for a minute and a half. Compactness, miniaturization. Cleanliness. The cross of modesty and prudishness called pudeur *in French. Brickwork. Class consciousness. Women of all ages suffering in skirts and stockings in the dead of winter. Reserve, aloofness, judgment. Varnished wood. Silent children, well-bred dogs, unassertive houseplants. The fear of God, the god of fear. Wallpaper. Comic strips. "Il faut cultiver notre jardin." The art of the display window, of undertaking parlors or cordwainers' shops, for example. A taste for scandal, especially morbid scandal. Kitsch. Africana. Flaccid pop music piped everywhere, including bookshops, hospitals, government offices. Leeks, chervil, gherkins, pickled onions. The ability to sit for long hours. White linen tablecloths, fanned linen napkins. Hammered brass. Tinted house windows. Symmetry. Monuments. The perpetual imminence of rage, blasphemy, running amok. Trees like fists. Rheumy eyes. Pale yellow, brick red, black.*—Luc Sante, describing his homeland of Belgium

How to Pen a Poetic List:
Moon on the floating boredom of rowboats
at Spirit Lake, Iowa, on flanks of somnambulist Guernseys
drifting the feedlots
and on the great burial mound outside Kahokia

Moon on the blue workshirts fingered by clotheslines,
on spin burnished into the sawmill's spare blade,
the crow's eye dismantled by ants,
the insomniac's watchband

Moon in chips in the bulldozer's gearshift knob,
on the black snake pausing at wheel ruts
and on the breathless steel mirror
nailed to the bathhouse door

Moon on Arizona butte-tops, their secret veins
of tourmaline, on cattle-guards marking access roads,
on breaks in the river, the island's fat leaves
and on the otter's nose, surfacing

Moon on rooftop antennae, the nightwatchman's key chain
and handcuffs, on the Art Institute's corridor wall
with 3 oils by Yves Tanguy

Moon on Ozark coondogs and the pair
of teenage brothers who follow, on aluminum crumples
tossed aside near the mouth to the cave
and on ash flaking over the campfire

Moon on nightcrawlers fattening golf greens
on the air's lathery riffles through cornfields,
on the widower's cigarette papers
and on the virgin lifeguard's legs, opening

Moon on the cable-car rails flowing up Telegraph Hill,
on the photographer's trip-wire baited
for owls, and on plastic tubing of lawn chairs
whose arms harvest dandelion fuzz

Moon on rake tines, the door-knocker's dolphin,
the planter's ceramic glaze leaking fern and on the white
white waitress barefooting it home from the bus stop
humming, dangling her sandals.
—Reg Saner, "Moon"

Turns out that Roy Orbison was not blind. It is true, though, that his first wife died in a motorcycle wreck and that two of his sons died in a house fire. He was Johnny Cash's neighbor.

My grandfather kept his boxing gloves on a hook near his bed, as if ready for business.

My mother bathed me in the tub before delivering me to the hospital where a Swiss doctor lanced my eardrum. Yellow pus sprang into the air, covering the doctor's sleeves. I may have been 11. My overnight roommate was a 17-year-old who was to die from kidney failure. I read in the paper that he'd been a pole-vaulting champion at Butte's Catholic high school, Central High. His hair was short, a brush cut.

I am, as many of you, a boomer of the 1946 sort. As of 2009, with my mother's death, I am officially a boomer orphan.

Rocky Marciano inhabits the same Florida mausoleum as my wife's mother.

In our home, there was plenty of aspirin and Vitamin C. Apples and turnips (and canned beets and peas) in the root cellar, a converted bomb shelter. My father had not finished pouring the concrete walls or installing the lead ceiling. The ventilation system remained what my father termed a *quandary*.

You may not be interested in war, but war is interested in you.
—Leon Trotsky

Long exiled from Butte, Evel Knievel died in 2007 in Clearwater, Florida, though not before he had accepted Jesus. As it turned out, he was

better known for his botches than his successes, with most of his primary jumps ending in damaging failure. When he neglected to land his jump at Caesar's Palace, he crushed his pelvis and femur, fractured his hip, a wrist, and both ankles. He looked like a bag of feed flopping on the concrete. The concussion kept him in a coma for 29 days. The plan to jump the Snake River Canyon was spawned, not surprisingly, in a bar. His funeral was conducted by the Reverend Robert H. Schuller of TV's *Hour of Power*. Evel is interred in the same cemetery as my parents.

Eddie Turner, Jackie Baker, and I lobbed dirt clods at Mrs. Lorango's wet sheets every wash day until we got caught. We were surprised that Mrs. Lorango knew we were the throwers and that our parents, without checking with us, believed her. We'd hid behind a berm in the cow pasture where we pretended we were pulling grenade pins with our teeth.

My father was a believer. That he was a devout Mormon, and the son of a failed one, was the thread of his cloth, the color his wool was dyed. Early on, I thought of him as armored. The chink I first recall was Sunday television. I was 9 or 10 when TV (with its three channels) arrived in Butte. The fat blond cabinet black-and-white seemed to pulse, even when switched off. I would have watched something—anything—every night. But in our house, homework and storybooks reigned, and Sabbath viewing was forbidden. One way or another, though, my father heard about the new Western *Gunsmoke*. As it turned out, my father's Sunday edict was subject to waiver. *Gunsmoke* became a long-running religious appointment, a sanctioned family event, behind drawn curtains.

Vernon Mackey was a retired miner who raised goats and calves. He was the person my father called whenever our cow gave birth or, in tearing through barbed wire, sliced her teats. He alone could milk our cow after she'd slashed herself. Hands caked with balm, he'd sing to the cow in Finnish.

Although my father promoted James Arness and his unwincing manliness as Marshal Matt Dillon, it seemed to me, even at my unperturbed age, that my father, although drawn to Dillon's qualities, was in love over his head with Miss Kitty, the single woman proprietor of the Long

Branch Saloon. My father was a breast man, a preference only aggravated when my mother later lost hers to a double mastectomy. She had been what was called, in those days of industrial bras, a *sweater girl*. In a photograph I recall, the wool features a moose and pine trees.

Mr. Mackey was at least 80 when he made a pass at my mom. "He pawed me!" she shouted at my father. To my ears, she wanted my father to confront the stick-limbed Finn but I could tell my father did not intend to. My father was a boxer. I knew what he could do if he thought he ought to. When Mr. Mackey invited my father to his property to take a sauna, he accepted and took me along. After we'd toweled, Mr. Mackey brought us ice-cold *Nesbitt's*, then tipped over our heads a couple of buckets of ice-cold water. He stood on a ladder to do this. We stood beneath him, balls shrinking.

Was my father aware that Miss Kitty had preceded him in death, that she'd died from complications from AIDS she may have contracted during a trip to Africa?

We owned a cow, an old Guernsey we kept in a bathroom-sized pen with a bathroom-sized shed in the backyard. The cow's name was *Pet*. When I milked Pet, she'd swing her shit-grimed tail. Pet's tail was a redhead's dirtied tresses encircling my neck and face, my ears and mouth. It was best to keep your trap shut. The idea I had was to shave the tail. Problem solved, I sat to milk. When Pet swung her tail, the rope of it nearly knocked me deaf. For a while I wore earmuffs and goggles.

My father's best friend Sidney died at Pearl Harbor. My father had tried to join up but had been denied enlistment because of a childhood mishap in his father's woodyard that had blinded one eye. My father had wanted to join the Navy before the attack on Pearl Harbor, explaining that if he and Sidney had been able to enlist together, they could have asked to be assigned to the same ship. Whatever would have happened to my father on board Sidney's ship would have happened more than four years before my birth.

The English language would be bereft without Shakespeare. Does it

matter to be certain of his identity—the son of illiterate parents, a closet Catholic, a man of the court? Shakespeare, on his own, added 21,000 words to English, in a world in which a typical French dictionary hardly contains 40,000 words.

Paroles.

Early morning Sunday was the service for men only, followed by Sunday school for all. The later afternoon was tied up for a final service, another combination gathering. After dinner we'd assemble for *Gunsmoke*. We came to know Doc Adams, the gimp-legged Chester, Festus, and even Burt Reynolds as the half-breed Quint. A child and survivor of the Great Depression, a willing boxer, a miner and woodsman, a reliable citizen, an ungrumbling husband and father, my father admired dependable men. He admired Marshal Dillon but he didn't seem to comprehend Dillon's on-screen discretion. He was certain Matt and Kitty were sleeping together. As a man who invited my mother for scheduled weekend naps behind a locked bedroom door, from which he emerged refreshed, often singing, I doubt my father itched for testimony of any coupling but he may have thought the marshal should have whistled or hummed. *Something.*

There was a mining engineer who would stomp through my father's mining office with his night crew. This engineer had taken to sitting in my father's chair and propping his cruddy boots on the desk. My father told him if he did this again he was going to knock him to the floor. I'd heard my father set forth the situation to my mother. My father worked Saturdays at the mine, above ground, for half days, and I often tagged along. In my father's office, I'd fiddle with ore samples (I'd assembled a labeled collection—pink manganese, cobalt, iron pyrite, quartz, zinc—in an egg carton for a Cub Scout badge), and sharpen pencils. Sometimes my father would let me wash up his respirators in a big sink and install clean filters. I'd draw with my father's drafting tools.

If you wish to scrawl in English—you have Shakespeare and an additional 150,000 words.

The Saturday I'm writing about, we entered the office to the engineer in my father's chair with his feet on the desk. When my father kicked the castored chair, the engineer and his elevated feet crashed to the floor. My father jutted his chin toward the slime on his desk, then handed the man a pair of red boxing gloves. He had removed two pair from his desk's bottom drawer. *Where had those come from?* I had not known that my father worked in a place where boxing gear was essential. Whatever the case, he educated the engineer that Saturday, conducting a clinic in fisticuffs. Right away he landed one on the nose—a quick flick with his shoulder behind it. And if the snapped nose hadn't diluted the big man's starch, what my father next did to his ribs did. The clinic was almost over before it started. Everything my sweet-tempered father did was exact and quick and vicious.

Fifty years and the picture sticks: *my father knocking icicles from the eaves with a broom.* It's the night before Christmas in Butte, Montana, where, in 1959, the miners are on strike, and here's my long-legged father, out of work, knocking on ice. My father has jerked the broom from a snowbank beside the carport—the carport he'd built the summer before with salvaged 4×4 posts and corrugated Fiberglas. The Fiberglas is a mint green that tints sun.

Donald Arthur Anderson is interred in Butte. His engraved name is shortened to Don A. Anderson, the way he signed it. After the burial, I returned to Colorado to a letter posted three days before the day my father died.

Dec 8, 1993
 Merry Xmas. We will put our tree up tomorrow. Your mother is go-ing with me today to buy one. It's been quite cold here but it's warmed up some. I can still start all my cars without plugging them in. Yesterday, it's been 52 years since my pal Sidney's boat sunk. How could I still miss him? We have new carpet in our kitchen, bath, and back porch. Our upright freezer finally gave up—we had to get a new one. We have 2-refrigerators, 2-freezers, 2-microwaves, 4-TVs, 4-phones. I think we are pretty well equipped, don't you?
 —All love. P.S. I've got to do something about the carport.

Oddjob is the Korean henchman, valet, and chauffeur to Auric Goldfinger of the James Bond film. Connery was my favorite Bond, depending, as he did, more on charm, self-possession, luck, and brawn, than on gizmos.

I can't help but see the carport, its paled Fiberglas, except for the nail holes, resisting weather, moths, rust, and time. This manufactured overhead product had outlasted my old man. I'd thought his shelf life would have pressed on, *like* Fiberglas, or gold, or copper, Styrofoam, sealed Twinkies, MoonPies, the sproutable wheat found in the tombs of Pharaohs.

A promoter of organ donation, my father, in the end, donated only the cornea from his one good eye. Remaining organs were discarded as *worn*.

There is a theory that a certain number of monkeys typing a certain number of years would eventually produce the complete works of Shakespeare, which I doubt because such a project isn't just a statistical problem.

1901. The Montana Legislative Assembly passes the "eight-hour day." Within three years, Butte claims the largest payroll in the world—12,000 men in the mines and mills with a payroll of $1,500,000 a month.

There were no policies against livestock in Butte. Because I so hated milking, I dreamed of the sheriff coming to our house to tell my father it was illegal to keep cows. I didn't hold out much hope because at school we studied Montana history and I knew there were more cows in my state than people, and my teacher had said that Montana statutes dictated death by hanging for cattle rustling, but not for human murder.

Homicide: From the Latin *homo* "man" + *caedere* "to slay."

Miss Stephanie, my fifth-grade teacher, whom I loved like my father loved Miss Kitty, was from California. She said San Francisco housed more people than our whole huge state, but then admitted that San

Francisco couldn't have penned all the cows. *Your* cows was the way she put it.

If it was my sisters who named our old Guernsey *Pet*, it was my father who named our new cow: *Marilyn*. He kept a pinup calendar in his bureau's top drawer. The twelve months of Miss Monroe confirmed a penchant for chests and black-mesh nylons. Old Pet had been put down and my father bought a two-acre field across from our house. Silver Bow Creek ran through the field. Encircled by barbed wire, the two acres featured a tin-sided shed, a manger, and a berm from behind which we lobbed our dirt clods at the wet sheets.

It was my job to shepherd Marilyn to the stockyards—a one-man, single-cow cattle drive. You want your friends to see you walking a cow to the stockyards to be bred? You're 16 years old. You live inside the city limits. In a fenced field across the street from your house is a cow your father wants humped. You're driving a cow with a stick in your hand. You're herding a cow with a stick to the stockyards.

The bull is let in. Cowboys materialize and arrange themselves all along and on the corral's top rails. The bull, short-legged, has a hard time reaching. There are jokes. When the bull connects, everyone cheers, so you nod your head, squint. Your father pays someone. You find your stick and start the cow for home. The old girl seems bedazed and druggy.

1867. Butte City is laid out and the population reaches 500. A Pony Express letter from Butte 85 miles to its sister gold camp of Virginia City costs 25 cents.

The closest I got to Vietnam was Beale Air Force Base near Yuba City, California: the placid, rural town where Juan Corona courted, then hacked and buried all those faceless, nameless, randomly hapless male fruit-pickers in the local peach orchards. Corona's 1971 work became the grisliest mass murder known to date in the United States. The week the 25 orchard graves were unearthed along the Yuba City banks of the Feather River, 29 GIs were killed by a North Vietnamese rocket at

Charlie Two, a tiny firebase near the Demilitarized Zone. The average weekly U.S. death toll in Vietnam that year was 49, down from a weekly average of 81 the year before.

Sometime during the nine minutes after the USS *Arizona* was initially struck, Sidney died. "Drowned," guessed my father. At 8:10 A.M., December 7, 1941, a 1,760-pound bomb pierced the deck of the ship to explode a fuel tank. Seven seconds later, when the forward ammunition magazines blew (1.7 million pounds of ignited gunpowder), heads and other human parts and random metal debris rained down on sailors and the seemingly steelier decks of adjacent ships. The few *Arizona* crewmen to survive swam to shore naked, their clothes stripped from them by the force of the ship's detonations. By 8:19 the *Arizona* had settled to the bottom of Wai Momi, as the early Hawaiians had titled the "pearl waters" of the harbor.

A summer of '46 birth, I supposed myself an emphatic consequence of armistice, my father and mother properly delaying my birth until their upheaved world became safe—*for me.* This dreamy version of my parents' decision about my conception seemed to me sound and true for years. Actual military events in Korea and French Vietnam and Hungary and Poland and the Suez seemed distant and unmournful as I confronted them from within the high-windowed walls of my schools through my *Weekly Reader.* Sputnik, though, and the discovered presence of Soviet ballistic missiles in nearby Cuba, quailed me. Weapons which could climb to space to descend unimpeded to earth pressured up dread, particularly when my father pondered aloud (during family meals) the constructing of an underground shelter, then actually began storing water in emptied Clorox jugs and our canned and dried foods in an interior room in the basement.

It was a predictable slide from *Gunsmoke* to *The Ed Sullivan Show.* Though both shows got their starts in 1955, and though both productions lasted years, Ed Sullivan changed America in ways *Gunsmoke* and the marshal did not. In Butte, there may have been Irish and Finns and Swedes and Czechs. There may have been Poles, Mexicans, Germans, Filipinos, Chinese, Italians, Indians—Blackfoot, Crow,

Assiniboine—and Welsh miners from West Virginia, but there were no blacks I knew of—none in my schools. What I learned about blacks, I learned from Ed Sullivan on Sundays, after church.

Draft lottery "#1" for the 1970 drawing is July 9: *my* birthday. I immediately join Air Force ROTC. My plan is to stay clear of the army (more soldiers being buried than airmen). And if forced to Vietnam, I mean to be forced there as a lieutenant—an *officer* in charge of his future. The month I sign up for the Air Force Reserve Officer Training Corps, the Pentagon releases to the public news of 34 deaths in 209 incidents in Vietnam of officer "fraggings"—that is, U.S. officers being attacked by their own soldiers. Attacks on officers by their own troops in time of war reached unprecedented proportions in Vietnam, with some historians reporting as many as 2,000 incidents a year.

A female air force captain, recently returned from Afghanistan, rightly spoke of the youth of the troops: "All they want to do is eat pop tarts and play video games and all we do is give them grenades."

Nietzsche understood that the trouble with war is that it induces stupidity in the victor and vengeance in the vanquished.

"Frag":
One of war's few privileges, this, after fragmentation grenade, is the verb for wounding or killing an unpopular officer in one's own unit. It was done in other wars, too, before we had a word for it. My father, a sergeant, was suspected of it in World War One, when a certain lieutenant suggested they go out into no-man's-land just to waste some time and give him an opportunity to write my father up for a decoration. "I don't care to have an undecorated senior NCO." My father came back unscathed and alone. The lieutenant's successor repeated the excursion, but had the same bad luck, and my father returned intact and undecorated, saying a sniper each time had fired on them. There was no third time: No officer could be found willing to take my father again into no-man's-land, lest he get fragged by whomever. Did German nighttime snipers kill officers only?
—Paul West

What to Do:
Don't talk to pit bull owners about pit bulls—they don't know what you're talking about.

At first, the blacks on Ed Sullivan's show seemed damaged: Sammy Davis Jr., who could dance but sported an immobile glass eye after he'd lost his mothered eye in a near-fatal car wreck. And: Ray Charles, who couldn't see at all, and who swayed when he sang in a way that looked uncurbed and chancy. I pictured Ray crooning in his shower, thwacking through glass.

The black women, by contrast, appeared whole, even larger than life: Mahalia Jackson, Pearl Bailey. Or sexy: The Supremes or Horne. Lena Horne. Lena Horne could sing, but unlike Pearl, Mahalia, even Diana, she could dance, and when she sang and danced it was a flirt apart from what I knew about. Following a particular Sunday night set, my father pronounced: *Pretty good looking . . . for a Negro.* What was wrong with what he'd said was not clear to me at my age then, but what I heard in my father's voice was as much wonder as cluttered admiration.

Warned not to attach my tongue to metal in Montana during winter, I began eyeing the galvanized posts on the grounds of a house I passed on my way to Emerson Elementary. The mercury registered 30 below when I chaperoned my experiment.

Artillery lends dignity to what might otherwise be a vulgar brawl.
—Frederick the Great

Because of his damaged eye, my father served (wearing safety glasses) in copper mines in Montana. The loss of battle in World War II always seemed to me a galling and double privation for Donald Arthur Anderson: he not only lost his best friend, he also missed his one good chance for war—grinding for a man who did not dodge fights or forget friends.

Although some 20 ships were destroyed or damaged (as well as most of the parked aircraft at all nearby airfields), the deaths inflicted upon the *Arizona* account for half of all U.S. casualties at Pearl Harbor.

Aboard this one vessel, 1,170 men died. Of this number, 1,102 remain entombed—below water, below deck. The average age of the ship's dead was 23. Among the ship's victims were 22 sets of brothers and uncounted sets of friends. Seventy percent of the ship's crew perished. Sidney's body was not recovered, though there is a headstone a short walk from where my father lies.

Stationed at Beale Air Force Base in California, I began to meet people who had served or were on their way to serve in Vietnam. For one, there was the marine corporal in a night class I enrolled in at Yuba City Community College. The corporal had come home from the war, mustered out of the corps after a voluntary second tour. In class, he read aloud the harsh, unrhymed, unmetered lines he wrote about death and Vietnamese women. "YEA, THOUGH I WALK THROUGH THE VALLEY OF THE SHADOW OF DEATH, I FEAR NO EVIL . . . 'CUZ I'M THE MEANEST MOTHERFUCKER IN THE VALLEY" was the silk-screened quote that read split on the front and the back of a T-shirt the corporal had made and brought home. Every time I saw him he was wearing the shirt. If you gazed his way, he would thump his chest and grunt. He was looking for fights.

Mammogram.

Colonoscopy.

His church's attitudes aside, my father was an unbound fan of Joe Louis, the "Brown Bomber." But it was Archie Moore my father admired most—that peculiar wiliness, that particular heart. My father took it personally when Marciano kayoed Moore. He couldn't even talk about the fight with Ali, then called Clay. He could about the battle with Yvon Durelle though. Floored three times in the first round in a ring in Montreal, and floored again in the fifth, Moore retained his title with a desolating blow in the 11th round. Archie was 45 at the time. The Canadian fisherman not yet 30.

We hear of, say, My Lai or Abu Ghraib, and want to believe—don't we?—that our choices would have been different from those who will

27

find their place in history as moral dwarves. Except: As the Milgram and the Stanford Prison experiments uncomfortably disclose—humans are only too willing to obey authority, even when that authority conflicts with their conscience. As we should by now know, it is in this way that ordinary folk, by merely "doing their jobs," become agents in persecution, "cleansing," and genocide.

Now and again during the Milgram experiments, someone would refuse to "obey," either to start or to continue to administer what they had every reason to believe was debilitating, if not fatal, electrical shock to unseen but screaming recipients. But such forswearing individuals were always in the minority.

My father advanced that Moore, with some 200 fights and the most knockouts ever (141!), was dodged for so long that when he first fought for the light heavyweight championship of the world, he was 39 years old. With dread and esteem in his voice, my father said Moore then defended that title for the next 10 years, the longest period in the division's history. As a light heavyweight, Moore fought for the heavyweight championship twice. And though he was kayoed by Marciano in nine rounds, he dropped the Rock with a sacking right in the second. Moore had begun his boxing career in 1935. By the time he fought Clay, Archie Moore was 50.

Had my first wife asked once more: *Is that a joke?*—I would have to have had her killed.

Regime change.

Argument:
Marry someone who thinks you're hilarious. Which counters my father's advice about broads: *Eat crow.* But he was the same man who advised, *If you have to fight a Negro, crack his nose. It takes the starch right out of them.*

Pretty good looking . . . for a Negro?

28

If you can't imagine yourself an SS officer hustling the Jewish women and children to the gas chamber, you need to be more closely in touch with your buried self. —Paul Fussell

Samuel Hynes heard a man at a dinner party suggest a solution for the siege of Sarajevo: "We could take those guns out with a little napalm." Hynes, a former marine pilot, thought, "You have never seen napalm dropped, you don't know how it flows and spreads like a wave of fire and burns *everything*." Hynes also records a French foot soldier from the First World War who said it this way: "The man who has not understood with his flesh cannot talk to you about it."

Nothing has changed.
The body is susceptible to pain,
It must eat and breathe air and sleep,
it has thin skin and blood right underneath,
an adequate stock of teeth and nails,
its bones are breakable, its joints are stretchable.
In tortures all this is taken into account.
—Wislawa Szymborska, from "Tortures"

Mission Accomplished. —George W. Bush

The trouble with Eichmann was precisely that so many were like him, and that the many were neither perverted nor sadistic, that they were, and still are, terribly and terrifyingly normal. From the viewpoint of our legal institutions and of our moral standards of judgment, this normality was much more terrifying than all the atrocities put together.
—Hannah Arendt

You can tell a true war story if it embarrasses you. If you don't care for obscenity, you don't care for the truth; if you don't care for the truth, watch how you vote. Send guys to war, they come home talking dirty.
—Tim O'Brien

An observant nineteenth-century cardiologist noted that a Civil War combatant's cardiovascular system could be altered by that soldier's battlefield experiences. Named for the cardiologist, "Da Costa's syndrome" manifests a set of symptoms like those of heart disease and anxiety, though a physical examination will not present physiological abnormalities. Perhaps because of its parallel psychological manifestations, "Da Costa's syndrome" became more commonly known as "soldier's heart." What with World War I's constancy of barrage on crammed trenches, the medical term for seemingly intact but maimed soldiers morphed into "shell-shocked" and "battle fatigue," to be followed by World War II's and Korea's familiar "thousand-yard stare." The term since Vietnam is, as we know, Post-Traumatic Stress Disorder, or PTSD.

Our current war's injuries, an odd consequence of effective body armor and blasts from explosive devices, are contributing as never before to "closed head wounds"—invisible damage contributing strenuously, as you might expect, to PTSD.

It is all practice: when we emerge from experience, we are not wise but skillful. But at what?—Albert Camus

My old editor at the National Geographic Adventure magazine used to be a Golden Gloves fighter in Ohio, and he was talking about the young interns they had working at the magazine. He said, "You know the trouble with a lot of these people, a lot of them have never been cut."
—Philip Caputo, qtd. in Herzog

My father told the story that when Sugar Ray Robinson tore apart Carl "Bobo" Olson for the middleweight crown, Archie Moore wired: *Ray—you preached a good sermon, and I think he got the word.*

Well, about my experience, it illustrates how you can become something you never thought you would become, without being aware of the transformation. That there is evil in you, or violence in you, or both—which you're not fully aware of—and that it can sneak up and in effect possess you, or snatch your soul."—Philip Caputo, qtd. in Herzog

The three of us crouched in the corner of the house, trembling and cry-
ing all at once, thinking that surely we would die here as the bullets and
shrapnel were destroying our small wooden home. We decided to leave
and find a safe place to hide. So we went through the back, through the
kitchen, my husband carrying our young daughter in his arms. A plane
flew very low and seemed to be coming directly at us and firing rockets
all over, striking my daughter in the back and my husband as he carried
her. From where I was, only a few paces behind them, I saw only the
heart and the entrails of my child. She seemed to have been blown apart,
completely destroyed. My husband stumbled some thirty steps with his
arms torn away, blood pouring out of him till he fell dead. There was a
great hole in his chest. Part of it was still smoking, a smoking rocket was
still in one leg. The other was stripped of all flesh to the bone. I wanted
to pick up my daughter, but there were only pieces of her. . . . I ran and
found her arm and tried to put it back on her, tried to put back everything
that had spilled out of her. But she was already dead. She was my only
child and it was hard for me to have her. I dressed her myself for parties.
Spoiled her. I don't know what I'm going to do.—Nicaraguan mother,
qtd. in Bowen and Weigl

It seems as if the less a writer has accomplished, the longer the contribu-
tor's note, the explanatory bio.

What Not to Do:
Saddle your kids with names like "Apple" or "Willow"—"Harley," "Hub-
cap," "Lug-nut," "China," "Bubbles". . .

Mother of a Nineteen-Year-Old Soldier Killed in Kirkuk:
It was the lightest tap on my door that I've ever heard in my life. I opened
the door and I seen the man in the dress greens and I knew. I immediately
knew. But I thought that if, as long as I didn't let him in, he couldn't tell
me. And then it—none of that would've happened. So he kept saying,
Ma'am, I need to come in, and I kept telling him, I'm sorry, but you can't
come in.—*New York Times,* November 12, 2004

Give Attention to Warnings:
If I have to stop this car. Fragile. You could lose an eye.

My mother was the 1943 typing champion of her high school in Deer Lodge, Montana.

August 2011. The world's last typewriter factory (Godrej and Boyce) closes its doors in Mumbai, India. No demand. Not even in India.

In an update to the August 2011 news report, a New Jersey-based company called Swintec reports continuing sales of typewriters being manufactured in China, Japan, and Indonesia. One model is encased in clear plastic so that contraband cannot be hidden inside, as a robust market for Swintec is prisons.

I got through college with a *Royal Futura Portable.* You?

What antique superstition stands behind the notion that damn and hell are bad words and that kill and murder are not? Certainly rape is a more obscene concept than fuck. Why then do we not consider it a more obscene word? —Edward Lueders

What I Learned in the Military:
Nothing is impossible to people who don't have to make it come true.

Best Contributor's Note:
John Updike lives in Massachusetts.

For a Meal of Sheep's Head:
Split head and remove eyes. Remove brain and soak in vinegar and water. Soak washed head in salted water. Blanch head. Boil (gently) brains. Scrape meat from head. Skin tongue and cut in slices. Add meat, tongue, and brains to white sauce. Reheat and serve with toast points and minced parsley.

Combat Zone Graffito:
Killing For Peace Is Like Fucking For Virginity

In 1987, I began suffering abdominal cramps of the serious sort. At the time a committed long-distance runner, I convinced my physician that

what I was experiencing was an exercise-induced electrolyte imbalance. He prescribed packets I poured into my water bottles. Medically trained, he counseled more fruits and vegetable.... On Memorial Day, my intestine burst.

A tested surgeon, who'd labored in Nepal without paperwork or fear of malpractice, cut me open to remove an arm's length of shredded intestine. "There was shit everywhere!" was the way he explained it. He'd flopped what he termed *everything* out to shower me down with a sterile saline solution. My colon was now stitched to an aperture in my belly. The surgeon pulled away the sheet to show me. The organ, if that's what it was, appeared to be breathing.

Battle is a great leveler of human aspiration when it most surely should not be. Stray bullets kill brave men and miss cowards. They tear open great doctors-to-be and yet merely nick soldiers who have a criminal past, pulverizing flesh when there is nothing to be gained and passing harmlessly by when the fate of whole nations is at stake. And that confusion, inexplicability, and deadliness have a tendency to rob us of the talented, inflate the mediocre, and ruin or improve the survivors—but always at least making young men who survive not forget what they have been through.—Victor Davis Hanson

The two-day incendiary raid by more than 2,000 Allied bombers ignited a firestorm that consumed the city of Dresden, claiming 135,000 German souls. The medieval Dresden was the home of Europe's first china. The making of pottery is an ancient art, though not overly ancient, because it requires a banked and tended fire. In firing, the moisture in the clay is removed.

Remember the Alamo. Remember Oppenheimer. *A woman without a man is like a fish without a bicycle.* Remember Steinem.

Father of a Twenty-Four-Year-Old Son, Dead in Iraq:
Don't use the word "closure" with me!

My wife's step-great aunt died in a nursing home where she had lived

in her own apartment. While settling her affairs we lived in that apartment, because the rent had been paid through the month and was not refundable.

What Will Not Occur in a Nursing Home Shower:
(1) You won't be scalded.
(2) You won't drown.

Character is determined by what one respects; the rest is a personality or style. Style is a matter of how you handle things. It is movement, touch, arrangement, speed, care, and carelessness, not just how you handle words, but how you pick up a child, pet a dog, or make and throw a snowball.
—Edward Lueders

In May 1963, Buddhists, demonstrating in Hue against persecution by the Diem regime, were fired on by government police. On June 11, a monk set himself aflame at a major intersection in downtown Saigon. This act, tipped off to an AP reporter, was recorded and the photo flashed about the world. The incident drew attention.

Combat Zone Graffito:
Mail Call Cancelled Until Morale Improves

. . . losing a parent is something like driving through a plate-glass window. You didn't know it was there until it shattered, and then for years to come you're picking up the pieces—down to the last glassy splinter.
—Saul Bellow

There is nothing oblivion won't forgive.—Mark Jarman

It is impossible to jaunt about, feeling cool and invulnerable, with a plastic bag of shit hanging from your gut.

Diverticula are abnormal pockets in the wall of the intestine. In about 20 percent of persons with diverticulosis, the diverticula become inflamed, and, in severe cases, there is bleeding and perforation of the

intestinal wall. Surgical removal of infected portions of the colon may become necessary.

What confused the doctor was that the presence of saclike herniations of the mucosal layer of the colon through the muscular wall is more common among older folks and not among younger ones who are active. It is why he bought my layman's electrolyte theory.

Lying abed and pumping morphine, I wanted to know how to avoid the reoccurrence of intestinal failure. *A high-fiber diet and exercise* is what the man who'd been to medical school said. I was 42, a marathon runner, and a vegetarian.

Some haystacks don't even have any needle.—William Stafford, "An Argument against the Empirical Method"

My idea of camping is sleeping in a place where the towels are thicker than the ones I have at home.

1963. John Kennedy's dead. Eight months later, in what seems an unknowable world, I register (within five working days of my eighteenth birthday) with the Selective Service. With that act, I become aware of a new factor in the situation of my possibly being in uniform: the United States is involved in Vietnam. Before Kennedy died, I find, he had positioned "advisers"—15,000 thousand—in Vietnam and had authorized hundreds of millions of dollars in aid. Our Jack in Vietnam? Had he thought he'd found a way to respond in safety to the hectoring Khrushchev?

Within weeks after I register with the Selective Service, U.S. aircraft begin bombing North Vietnam. Seven months later (March 8, 1965), U.S. Marines land at DaNang. By December 1965, there are 200,000 American soldiers on the ground (replacing "advisers"), a figure that takes but one year to double. By the following Christmas, December 1967, there are 500,000 U.S. soldiers assigned to Vietnam—*12 times* the population of any city I've ever yet lived in, *50 times* the 10,000 students enrolled at the state university I then attend.

1968. The USS *Pueblo* is seized by the North Koreans. The Tet Offensive begins. The chairman of the Joint Chiefs of Staff announces the request for additional soldiers (200,000 *more* is what Westmoreland asks his boss for). Martin Luther King Jr. is murdered. Robert Kennedy is murdered. Fear and peril feel yeasty, viral. A small victory: Westmoreland is refused the request for 200,000 new soldiers, though he does command, by year's end, 540,000—the additional 40,000 representing for me every resident of Butte, the city I was raised in. Nonetheless, this reduction in U.S. military reinforcements I accept as personal relief, for as 1968 closes, there is hard talk of a draft lottery and termination of all college deferments.

GI Latrine Graffito, Saigon:
Withdrawal is something Nixon's father should have practiced 58 years ago

A's hire A's; B's hire C's.

Nothing beats an argument from personal experience.—Milan Kundera

If you were blind, would you be in love with a different person?

When I was a kid at Emerson Elementary, there were inflexible drills during which we ducked under our desks (pushing our own heads with our own hands toward the floor), as if the drawn blinds and our desks and our suppliant positions would have saved us from nuclear doom.

Napalm is a petroleum gel that is ignited by contact and burns prolongedly. Because napalm is a jelly, it affixes to what it burns. Napalm was developed by Harvard University scientists.

We are unique only in very limited ways and usually only when we're in love.

An estimate of the force of the firestorm in Dresden can be obtained by analyzing it as a meteorological phenomenon: as a result of the sudden linking of a number of fires, the air above is heated to such an extent that a violent updraft occurs, which, in turn, causes surrounding fresh

36

air to be sucked in from all sides. This suction causes movements of air far greater than normal winds. In meteorology, the differences of temperature involved to create wind current are on the order of 20° to 30°C. In the Dresden firestorm, the temperature differences were on the order of 600° to 1000°C. This explains the liveliness of firestorm winds.

The name the writer presents to the world is determining—i.e., *Billy Collins*. Is this the name for a poet laureate or a second baseman just traded to the Twins?

I knew Doris Day before she was a virgin.—Oscar Levant

William Collins? Wm.? W. Collins?

The year I qualified for Social Security, I deep-sea fished. In Florida waters, I hooked a sailfish the height and size of a slimmed Wilt Chamberlain. Catching a sailfish is like snagging a mattress that can swim. Sailfish cut through water up to speeds of 70 mph. Predictably, I reread *The Old Man and the Sea*.

After the sailfish, the bonita seemed as seaworthy and heavy as bowling balls.

Rereading *Moby Dick* would have seemed pretentious.

What is sadder than illiteracy except Ebola, dirty bombs, tumors, drowning . . .

Addiction.

Billy "Boom-Boom" Shakespeare: the undefeated, undisputed heavyweight champ and pound-for-pound writer . . .

1910. Carrie Nation, the temperance crusader, visits Butte and is ejected from a Galena Street bagnio by an irate madam.

Soweto.

Gulag.

I did not talk to the blue-finned fish or think of it as my *brother*—
actually, I kept hoping for the line or the hook to snap. After an hour,
I managed to reel the fish close enough for the boat captain to tag it
and then release. The catch was recorded so that, in theory, should the
fish be caught again, I'll be informed by email. The captain grabbed the
sailfish by its sworded bill to steady it for the tagging.

My brother Ross had lived, but had not come home. My mother's breasts
were removed not long after the subdued funeral. What I remember
is my mother in bed or shuffling furniture and appliances to wax the
house's linoleum floors. Floors hidden by a sofa or fridge, shone. We
had ironed clothes and clean sheets, a waxed floor, and cracked wheat.
My mother could sing harmony, a sweet alto. She was a seamstress. One
Halloween I was Zorro, and I'd been an outfitted gunslinger, a knight,
and a pirate. One year I was a robot in a costume I'd made myself of
empty boxes. I spray-painted over *Zenith, Del Monte, Jack Daniel's.*
When I walked, I'm sure I looked addled or drunk—stiff-legged, stiff-
necked, stiff-backed—a squat human housed in discarded cartons.

How to Name a Rock Band (A–Z):
Acid Reign
Blind Melon
Country Joe and The Fish
Drive She Said
Electric Prunes
For Selena and Sin
Glamour of the Kill
High Watt Electrocutions
Ignominious Incarceration
Jooz Gizzi
Knifeworld
Lucky Punch
Mojo Gurus
Nightwish
Operation Mindcrime

Prudas Jeist
Quartz
Reef
Spooky Tooth
Type O Negative
Unruly Child
Viking Skull
Winnebago Deal
Xcerts
You and What Army
Zodiac Mindwarp

More rock bands have named themselves starting with *S* than with any other letter—that is, unless you count the prefix *The* as confirming the letter *T*. Otherwise, *S* wins.

Firebombing in Japan during World War II was in particular effective, but required many bombers and many bombs. A firebombing sortie called for up to as many as 300 bombers, each carrying, at war's end, an average of 7.4 tons of bombs. Enola Gay, by contrast, carried one crew and one bomb over Hiroshima. "Little Boy," the atomic bomb lowered on Hiroshima, was the approximate size of a 10-foot man weighing 9,000 pounds. "Little Boy" killed 70,000 people.

"Fat Man" wasn't scheduled for Nagasaki. About the same length as "Little Boy," though rounder and heavier, "Fat Man" was to be air-burst above Kokura, but weather preserved the city. The Superfortress spent 10 minutes over Kokura without sighting its aim point, then proceeded to the secondary target of Nagasaki. Though the plutonium-based "Fat Man's" destructive potential exceeded that of the uranium-based "Little Boy," the hilly terrain of Nagasaki restricted damage: a few over 30,000 expired.

The day my father retired, he dubbed it a *privileged* occurrence. *Buoyant*. The man worked on his vocabulary, memorized poems, particularly those that rhymed. Fond of Longfellow and Robert Service, he could by heart quote "Hiawatha" and "The Cremation of Sam McGee."

He eschewed games like *Scrabble* or *Boggle* and puzzles of the crossword sort as if these were trivial means to acquiring language. Context was his game, though, in contradiction, when he gave me books to read—Edgar Rice Burroughs (*Tarzan and Mars*), James Oliver Curwood (*grizzlies and Canadians*), Booth Tarkington (*Penrod and friends*)—he advised that should I come upon words I didn't know to just skip them. I recall no dictionary in the house.

Polio.

In a story, a woman the main character means to marry doesn't arrive from the Eastern Seaboard. When the main character calls her, she inventively explains: "I'm sitting on the floor, surrounded by boxes but I can't seem to put anything in them."

Oh.

My mother owned a blue-covered copy of Shakespeare, thumb-tabbed to each play. She read, too, religious novels like Lloyd C. Douglas's *The Robe* and Lew Wallace's *Ben-Hur*. Published in 1880, *Ben-Hur* outsold *Uncle Tom's Cabin* and held title to all-time bestseller until *Gone with the Wind*. Lew Wallace was a Union general in the Civil War who later governed the New Mexico Territories. Lloyd C. Douglas was a minister. You know Clark Gable and Charlton Heston. Did you know that Ben-Hur's first name was Judah?

According to his wife, on the day my brother shot himself, he'd received his second delivery of morphine patches. An unfulfilled goal for Jimmie was to write the definitive text on how to hunt, prepare, and cook up duck. Jimmie is buried in Idaho.

In 1962, I tried to quit high school to work in a car wash. I'd wanted to work in the mines, but hadn't yet aged the required 18 years. My father promised to get me on at the Mountain Con (where he was then the safety engineer) as soon as I graduated from Butte High. I wanted to buy a car, had my eye on a 1947 Pontiac Silver Streak, the two-door. My father said I couldn't quit school; he said I could drive the Hudson.

The Hudson was a 1949 black-and-white two-tone that my father had formed with an axe and a hacksaw into what he thought passed as a half-ton truck. After he'd removed the back seat to connect the space with the trunk, he folded the roof to contain the front seat. He'd bent the roof by ramming it like a fullback, a pulling guard. He hacked a hole for a Plexiglas rear window and metal-screwed everything as tight as he could. During winter, the heater had to hump to keep the cab heated. The finishing touch was quarter-inch sheet metal welded to the frame for the truck bed. There was no tailgate. My vision of normalcy had been to pack Twinkies and Wonder Bread into my school lunchbox and to not ride about in a half-baked truck. What I took in my lunchbox was homemade bread—hand-milled wheat—and bulk carrots and apples my father bought then kept fresh by storing them in sand in the cellar. I'd seen pickups with tailgates that hinged flat to open and to extend the bed, and fancied my uncle's pickup, the word FORD embossed on the zinc-gray steel. The tailgate was unblemished, as if it'd never been touched or opened. Uncle Ken had threaded the tailgate chains with lengths of garden hose to stop the links from rattling, from nicking the paint.

In the living room, Christmas Eve, my father announces that before morning we need to know what a strike means. It's important to him that we digest that he is part of *management* and not *labor*. That is, he says, he's a *salaried* man, and not a man who shows up—drunk or sober—in the rustling line to hope for work for the day. The reason, he says, is because he has had two years of college. My father next advances the point that I will get four years of college and a stamped diploma. He informs my sisters that he will, when the time arrives, spring for a year of college at a Mormon school, *Ricks or Snow College, even BYU. Time enough to corral a stallion. But you*, he says, now pointing to me, *it's the full four years*. He tells me I may have to get a job to do it. I tell him I can get a job at the mine. *That's fine*, he says, *you'll have to*. At the time, I'm 13, and my sisters are 14 and younger. My baby brother is 6. In 40 years, he'll be dead, and it will be alcohol that takes him. In the 70s, AWOL from the army and jailed in Alberta for having beaten senseless an off-duty Royal Canadian cop, Jimmie, released from prison, rides a horse south. He had named the horse "Junction." Jimmie will visit me

41

in Colorado the year before he dies, but on Christmas Eve 1959, he is a six-year-old who has just started school.

sauce, shine, toddy, cups, solvent, swill, grog, sup, shot . . .

My brother James Arthur II, named for my grandfather, will not attend college. He'll spend some time in the army and in prison. He'll become a diesel mechanic and a master welder—his specialty custom horse trailers. He's a horseman too, supplementing his income by breaking broncos. Jimmie is 17 when I first see him handle a rough mount. As I think of it now, the performance makes me think of words like *id, bygone,* or *Hun.* The mare's flanks are roweled bloody and the specialized bit splits flesh. It is all clot and froth and lather.

bashed, fuddled, crocked, flushed, glazed, sizzled, laced, lit, fried, potted, sloshed, stewed, bladdered, lashed, tanked, tight, totaled . . .

My father is sweeping icicles because we are about to make ice cream. *It's damned cold,* which is not the way I would have put it then, little Mormon boy that I was. When I was a kid in Butte, winter temperatures often fell to 30, 40, even 50 below. It's cold and my father and I are in our sheepskins and lined, buckle-up overshoes. Snow is at our knees.

1938. A freak spring snowstorm paralyzes Butte. Snow falls for 80 hours.

Yes, the newspapers were right: snow was general all over Ireland. It was falling on every part of the dark central plain, on the treeless hills, falling softly upon the Bog of Allen and, farther westward, softly falling into the dark mutinous Shannon waves. It was falling, too, upon every part of the lonely churchyard on the hill where Michael Furey lay buried. It lay thickly drifted on the crooked crosses and headstones, on the spears of the little gate, on the barren thorns. His soul swooned slowly as he heard the snow falling faintly through the universe and faintly falling, like the descent of their last end, upon all the living and the dead.—James Joyce

Baghdad Bridge Graffito:
I will kell you, American

My father gets back to the business of the strike, now five months in tow. He, a *salaried* man, is on half pay. The miners, by contrast, are unemployed. Nonetheless, he says, we—*our* family—have had to *stretch*, gesturing at what I think he means us to see as the roof of our house, the electric lights that burn, the heat rushing from the vents above the furnace. He does everything but rub his stomach. He has told us stories of his father and the Great Depression. *We were never hungry. We had lousy clothes, but we ate. My father saw to it. So.* Our father points at us. Ordering us to knees, he prays his 1959 Christmas prayer about the wise men and the baby Jesus and all the angels and the animals around the smelly manger. We had a cow and a barn. Around cows, sterile straw is not easy to come by, hardly something the coming of wise men can change. I think this, but keep quiet.

Gout.

> "*They're trying to kill me,*" *Yossarian told him calmly.*
> "*No one's trying to kill you,*" *Clevinger cried.*
> "*Then why are they shooting at me?*" *Yossarian asked.*
> "*They're shooting at* everyone," *Clevinger answered.* "*They're trying to kill everyone.*"
> "*And what difference does that make?*"—Joseph Heller

On Christmas morning 1959, my sisters and baby brother and I each receive an orange and wrapped books. Some friends of our parents have donated their grown children's library. I get the entire *Bomba the Jungle Boy* set.

What People Say:
Below you will find the complete and unabridged record of the general conversation of the general public since time immemorial:
a. Hi, how are you?
b. I did not.
c. Good. Now you know how I felt.
d. Do you mind if I go ahead of you? I have only this one thing.
—Fran Lebowitz

Jean Piaget, the great child psychologist, claimed that his earliest memory was of nearly being kidnapped at the age of two. He remembered sitting in his baby carriage, from where he watched his nurse defend herself against the kidnapper. He recalled scratches on the nurse's face and a police officer with a short cloak chasing the kidnapper off. The policeman swung a white baton. The rub of the story is that the event had not occurred. Years after, Piaget's nurse confessed that she'd fabricated the event. Piaget later wrote that he must have heard, as a child, the account of this fabrication and projected it into the past in the form of a visual memory. It was, then, a memory of a memory, only false.

Studies have shown that there is no significant correlation between the subjective feeling of certainty a person has about a memory and that memory being accurate.—Daniel L. Schacter

Writing is not apart from living. Writing is a kind of double living. The writer experiences everything twice. Once in reality and once more in that mirror which waits always before or behind him.
—Catherine Drinker Bowen

"It's a poor sort of memory," Lewis Carroll's Queen says, "that only works backwards."

Russell Banks once pointed out to me that if all we wanted from one another was information then all we'd need to do is exchange drivers' licenses.

What to Do:
Give your love a cherry that has no stone.

Eyewitness accounts in court are, as a matter of course, granted less force than circumstantial evidence.

What every writing teacher must eventually tell her students: *Because something happened to you does not make it art necessarily.*

Before we made fire, before we made tools, before we made weapons, we made images. Art, at its deepest, is about preserving the world.

1937. January 15. The temperature in Butte registers at 40 degrees above zero. January 19. The temperature registers at 40 degrees below zero.

. . . There are strange things done in the midnight sun
By the men who moil for gold;
The Arctic trails have their secret tales
That would make your blood run cold;
The Northern Lights have seen queer sights,
But the queerest they ever did see
Was the night on the marge of Lake Lebarge
I cremated Sam McGee.
—Robert Service, "The Cremation of Sam McGee"

If Life and Art weren't different, we wouldn't need Art. We could just walk around with camcorders.

Fear of losing a woman and loving her are not the same thing.
—Russell Banks

Entr'acte
The woman was so small—the height and size of a three-year-old—that the clerk behind the Starbucks counter in the Cincinnati Airport didn't see her. When the clerk asked for my order, I, along with a hand gesture, said, "I believe she was first." Was I trying to pretend it was normal for a grown person to be 30 inches tall? The clerk—bless her heart—then leaned over the counter. To be fair, it was a wide counter, though I don't think higher than standard.

"Oh," the clerk said. "What would you like?"

"A small latté," the dwarf said.

The clerk, taller than I, was a thin black girl with straightened hair. She was kind and probably some years younger than the white dwarf below her.

When the clerk set the latté on the counter to reach for the money, she inadvertently set the cup beyond the dwarf's reach. The clerk handed over the change, then asked for my order. I pointed at the cup.

What was I feeling? Shame? Fear? Pride? Generosity? What I knew for sure was that whatever the feeling was, it was anchored in an awkward self-centeredness. What did this woman's growth have to do with me?

The clerk saw she had to push the latté closer, and she did. I ordered a small latté. I didn't want to give the impression that my body could absorb more liquid than the dwarf's. Besides, how to say Starbucks's word for small: *tall*?

The woman had to reach as high as she could to remove the plastic lid from her cup to add sugar. She'd moved down the counter, sliding the capped cup toward the stirrers, the honey and sugars. I was worried she'd pull the hot cup over onto her head—her uplifted face—and had to resist helping. Craning, she managed to add raw cane sugar, stir the coffee, and replace the lid. When she headed off in her little beige London Fog, navy slacks, and kids' clogs, I noticed her hands were the size of a woman's, strong and dexterous enough to hold her latté and to maneuver her rolling luggage. If her clothes were doll-size, her pull luggage wasn't.

For her height and size, her head was, as seems the case for dwarves, disproportionate. Too large, of course, but in this case—her case—only slightly. And her features were fine, not distorted. Her long hair was tended and highlighted professionally with streaks of blond.

I boarded my plane. Late that night, I told my wife about the little woman and her latté.

"She had glorious hair—really—I have to say," I say to Ellen. "A little kid's voice but a grown-up's hair. Luxurious. And she was neat and urbane in her kids' clothes, her little purse."

"You don't have to feel bad for her," my wife says. "Why do you feel bad? You feel bad, don't you? You do."

"Well, God," I say, "I think of Marnie racing her bike in that mountain thing in Moab." Marnie is one of our daughters. As the local joke goes, you can tell she's from Boulder, Colorado: She owns a $500 car, but pedals a $3,000 bicycle made from space-age metals.

"When I saw the little woman walking away," I say, "pulling that

suitcase her size, I thought about Marnie talking about her bike's composite frame, the composite shifters, titanium gears, step-in pedals."

I say: "Her feet lock into her pedals like ski boots. That little woman will never ride a mountain bike. They don't make good bikes that small. She'd have to buy a tricycle for Christ's sake—a goddamn Big Wheel or something. You know?"

"Why is this personal?" Ellen asks. "Is this personal?"

"I don't know."

"Dwarves attend conferences. I've read about this," Ellen says. "They have dwarf stores for clothes and furniture. Car stuff. A lot of dwarves drive cars." Then: "Dwarfism is treated as a disability. There are lobbies for this. 'Little People' lobbies. And conferences. She was probably on her way to a conference. They meet at these places, fall in love, marry, have babies."

"What kind of babies? Regular or small?"

"Regular," she says.

"Why would they be regular? A bald guy's son is usually bald. Big noses run in families. A son of an alcoholic is an alcoholic risk. A fat woman's mother is generally large, right? You think I didn't check out your mother?"

My wife is a slender woman who smokes cigarettes. She walks four miles a day. Power-walks. To stay fit, is what she says, and to keep on smoking. My wife buys cheap filtered menthols she stubs out when half-puffed. It stunts your growth, she says. I call her E sometimes instead of Ellen.

"You should quit, E," I say.

"You like tiny women," she says, lighting up. She raises a kitchen window and sticks her head close. She is a polite smoker insofar as she keeps smoke out of people's faces and houses, even her own.

"Why wouldn't dwarves bear dwarves?" I ask. And when Ellen doesn't answer: "What would a dwarf do with a four-year-old who could knock her over?"

Ellen blows smoke out the window, then swivels her head. "What makes you think all dwarves are actors or circus freaks?"

"I think that?"

"Do you?"

I say that every few years you read in the paper about dwarf-tossing

or such. "You don't remember Cuomo signing legislation banning dwarf-tossing and dwarf-bowling in New York bars?" We'd lived in New York for a few years.

"Dwarf-bowling?" E says.

"Yes."

"Bowling?"

"They strap them on skateboards and fire them down the lane." Then: "As I understand it, they do wear helmets and the pins are plastic."

I clamp shut because I suddenly remember seeing on TV some little folks wrapped in Velcro clothes. They were hung like pictures on Velcro walls. I don't recall whether they were tossed at the walls, but, in any event, I don't bring it up.

"Bars and bowling alleys," E says. "I take it they throw dwarves in bars."

"Liquor's involved," I say. "It would have to be, right?"

"You tell me," E says.

"Some dwarves have sued for the right to be tossed and bowled." I nod my head to enforce the point.

"Claiming what—the right to make a living?"

"So, maybe there should be a right? I mean, who stops 300-pound blubber boys from squashing skinnier backs and wide-outs? Why isn't that illegal? Pitchers fire balls at batters' heads. We're not talking hockey or Tyson eating Holyfield's ear. Consenting dwarves," I say, "wear sturdy little helmets and padding, and when they're tossed, they land on mattresses—no, usually a pile of them."

"Consenting? Did you say *consenting*?"

"I did." Then: "I say if a man wants to juggle hatchets, let him do it."

"Where would you draw the line," E asks, "—chainsaws, grenades, white phosphorus? White phosphorus," she says, "reacts rapidly with oxygen, catching fire at 10 to 15 degrees above room temperature. Dangerous enough, Ace?"

My wife takes a drag on her cigarette. She blows smoke into the room then shoots me a look. It's the look I imagined on the writer Annie Dillard's face a few years back.

I've never met Ms. Dillard, but have taken pleasure in her work and had just finished her book, *For the Time Being*. It's hardly a book in an obvious sense of unity and purpose. It is a loose yet rich federation

about human abnormalities, sand, clouds, numbers, China, Israel, God, evil, archaeology, and life-size Chinese clay soldiers and their horses—thousands of them sculpted for, then buried with the Emperor Qin to honor and protect him for the past 2,000 years. The clay soldiers and their mounts were a whole new idea. It had been the practice to bury an emperor's living army with him when he passed.

In the book, Dillard not only covers a variety of human abnormalities—noting, in particular, mentally deficient bird-headed dwarves—but a variety of human cruelties as well, such stunted acts as the flaying of the 85-year-old Rabbi Akiva for teaching Torah. The Romans, more than 100 years before Christ, stripped the rabbi's living flesh to its bones with horse currycombs, all the while the rabbi singing the Shema, *Hear O Israel, the Lord our God, the Lord is One.*

When I talk about the look on the writer's face, I'm thinking of a look that must have accompanied a one-sentence paragraph three quarters of the way into the book. Dillard, a smoker, notes: *Do you think I don't know cigarettes are fatal?*

In her book, for every heartening note such as seventeenth-century Jews who so respected books that when books wore out, they were buried like a person, there is a person like Joseph Stalin who took the long view: "One death is a tragedy; a million deaths are a statistic." Or Mao who told Nehru that the atomic bomb was nothing to be afraid of. Or a Ted Bundy who, with an invested sense of chilled proportion, is able to explain his serial killings: "I mean, there are so many people."

When I finally get into bed, Ellen is asleep. I lie on my back, eyes wide. What I see is my dwarf careening down a boulder trail in Utah. It's a full-size bike. There are metal extenders strapped to her feet and locked into her pedals. At times, as she flies down the trail, she's airborne. In this picture I'm painting, my dwarf is unhelmeted, her streaked locks like some nation's flag. But, as my eyes adjust to the bedroom's dark, my picture dissolves. I'm past 60 and I lie on my back thinking about college some 40 years before and the fraternity I joined. It was a group known for drinking and for reliable and current exam files. The president of the fraternity didn't live in the house on Greek Row. He bought one of his own, a three-story deal where he lived with eight roommates who covered his mortgage each month. I was one of the renters. "Grog" Robinson was, during his junior and senior years,

the Bareback Bronco Riding Champion in collegiate rodeo. He was better known, though, for the annual Frat Bash, which featured competitive dwarf-tossing.—"Stunted"

I should tell you that my wife heard me read this essay at a conference in Key West. After the reading: "I didn't say those things." "I know," I said, "but you could have." And there you have the hazard—on both sides—of having a writer in the house. In my defense, there were people in the audience who know both Ellen and me, and who said, "Sounds just like you, Ellen." I should report too, I suppose, that Ellen was hardly amused.

"Imagination," James McConkey has written, "is rightly seen as the creative power, the power that enables us to see affinities, to link disparate materials together in our search for a structure or form that will satisfy a personal sense of truth."

Why is it that as men grow older and wider they persist in buying the same waist-size jeans, then wearing them lower, cuffs bunching at the ankles? And: Do they think they can save the look with larger buckles?

Annie Dillard has called James McConkey's *Court of Memory* the non-fiction masterpiece of the 20th century.

History: Who can riffle through centuries and be sure?

Graham Greene: . . . *innocence is like a dumb leper who has lost his bell, wandering the world, meaning no harm.* David Keplinger: *The smell of a man's hat—an old man's hat—is like the nostril of a horse.* Jean Cocteau, in coming upon stacks of Marcel Proust's notebooks after Proust's death: . . . *watches ticking on the wrists of dead soldiers.*

A professor friend may be plagiarizing when he says *academics have more fears than medieval peasants*, but the line sounds trusty enough to steal.

William Burroughs was for thieving and against paraphrasing altogether.

Humility is no substitute for a good personality.—Fran Lebowitz

In 1962, when I intended to quit high school to work full-time in a car wash, I informed my father of my plans. He informed me of his. Two years after, public high school diploma in hand, I started college. My announced major was engineering—the degree my father would have sought had he had the reasonable fortune to skip an alcoholic father, the Depression, rheumatic fever, sleeping sickness, copper mines, a blinded eye, and an early family.

What I remember from first-year calculus is my professor, Mr. Smith— "Call me *Mister*, not *Professor*." Then: "Doctors repair worlds. They don't dismantle." He'd worked on the periphery of the Manhattan Project— knew Edward Teller, he said, Oppenheimer, Enrico Fermi. Mr. Smith was a drunk. One day he arrived late for class, selected a chalk, and began a white line, waist-high across the board. When he came to the end of the board, he continued. In fact, he drew a line across the windows and around the room. At the doorway, by which he'd entered, he turned. "Even that's not infinity," he said, then cast a lenient but morose look, then left. After one year of college, I, too, departed. For France, where I stayed three years. I did learn French, but when I returned home and to school, my new major was English.

Crick or creek?

Mayhap is archaic for *maybe* or *perhaps* or *perchance*, and appears in the dictionary near Mayo, as in the brothers William James and Charles Horace Mayo who founded the clinic of this name. One born at the beginning of the Civil War and the other at its end, they both died in 1939, the year, of course, that Germany invaded Poland. In 1939, my father was 19.

Rasputin's children?

Dag Hammarskjöld.

51

Combat Zone Graffito:
When In Doubt, Empty Your Magazine!

. . . We were busy fortifying Saida when some merchants appeared at our camp with news that a Tartar host had captured Baghdad. . . . After the city had been surrounded the Tartar chief sent to the caliph, saying he would like to arrange marriage between their children. The caliph agreed, however reluctantly, because he did not think Baghdad was strong enough to withstand a siege. The Tartars asked him to send forty members of his council who would swear to this marriage. He complied. Then he was asked to send forty notable citizens who would stand surety. This, too, he did. Now the Tartars would have forty more, chosen from the wisest men at court. Again the caliph did as they requested. And the Tartar chief, having got all these important men in his grasp, lopped off their heads. Next he assaulted and took the city because he knew that without their leaders the people would not put up much resistance. We were told that he held the foolish caliph in an iron cage and for a long time gave him almost nothing to eat. Then he asked if the caliph was hungry. The caliph replied that he was nearly dead of starvation. The Tartar placed before him a gold dish full of jewels and asked if he recognized them. I do, said the caliph, because they were mine. . . . Eat them, the Tartar said. They are not food, said the caliph. Now listen to me, said the Tartar. Had you bestowed this useless treasure upon your men they would have given their lives to defend you.—Evan S. Connell

All the time I was enrolled in ROTC, I believed I had, in an acceptable way, dodged war. But when I received my first ROTC check ($100 a month), I felt bothered enough to donate the sum to the American Red Cross. But I needed the money, so after giving away the first check, I began to keep them. I did, though, donate blood every six weeks or so when the Red Cross set up to collect in the gym. All-Service ROTC classrooms were housed in the same building as the gym, and every-one knew the blood collected was being shipped to Southeast Asia. I donated the blood (drank the Tang, ate the Oreos), and tried not to chafe at the Marine ROTC midshipmen who would arrive in noisy squads, an enthusiastic arrangement which allowed for competition as to which midshipman could fill his blood bag soonest. These in-embryo

Marines brought handballs to squeeze and clipboards and charts and stopwatches. I worried for the Marine midshipmen then, as I would worry for them now: they could hardly wait to give blood.

To die for an idea is to set a rather high price on conjecture.
—Anatole France

There is a certain impertinence in allowing oneself to be burned for an opinion.—Ibid.

The power of the atomic bomb comes from the forces holding each atom of substance together.

It is *not* the work of art to *make* order, but to *complicate* order in such a way that it resembles living . . .

Once you're in the field, the argument has passed clean through the "politics" of the discussion. You were standing in the middle of an awful nightmare. Politics had nothing to do with it. First things first, cousin. No, we were completely focused on making it through the night. A ghetto mentality. . . . The war was fucked up, that was clear. We were not very sophisticated about the rightness or the wrongness of the war, but everybody did know that it was bullshit. The lieutenants knew, the captains knew. When our new platoon leader, the one lieutenant I had any regard for, came into the platoon in the fall of '67, he had the NCOs, the track commanders meet. He looked at us and said, "Gentlemen, our job is to make sure everybody goes home in one piece." And we looked at him and said, "Lieutenant, this is an excellent plan; how can we help you?" And just like that we stopped doing ambushes; we stopped doing a lot of crazy, just-looking-for-shit-to-do stuff. There was a lot of just hanging back, lots of convoys. Meanwhile, we were, of course, headed straight for the Tet Offensive of 1968. Not fun. I should have come home in a bag.
—Larry Heinemann, qtd. in Herzog

1917. Frank Little, a member of the executive board of the IWW in Butte to organize a union, is hanged from a railroad trestle by armed masked men, who are never apprehended.

53

0 g trans-fat.

Hermann Baumann.

Although Mengele's subjects could be operated on without any painkillers at all, a remarkable example of Nazi zoophilia is that a leading biologist was once punished for neglecting to give worms enough anesthesia during an experiment.—Diane Ackerman

Garrotting earthworms.—Paul West, on literary criticism

At 5:46 A.M., January 17, 1995, Japan's worst earthquake in 50 years struck Kobe. Registering 7.2 on the Richter scale, Kobe's surface shimmied for 20 seconds, killing more than 5,000 people. That same week, following more than a full month of effort, the Russian army was effectively erasing Grozny, the Chechen capital, from the surface of the earth.

Beginning January 17, and for a week thereafter, the morning radio news brought ever-mounting Japanese death tolls and damage estimates. Interspersed among reports from Japan were on-site reports from the outskirts of Grozny. I heard a live report from a stone hut in the hills outside the capital. A peasant couple had gathered a number of children from Grozny and had brought them to the hut to escape the bombing. Also in the hut: a pregnant woman who, assisted by the older woman, was birthing a child. Over the voice of the radio reporter, you could hear the new mother scream, the children cry, and the unimpeded Russian bombers overhead, on track to their targets.

Do you think I don't know cigarettes are fatal?

Many of the Warsaw Zoo's animals were shipped by the Nazi leadership to purify their breeding. One high Nazi zoo official was in particular interested in back-breeding projects that would reintroduce European forest bison and superior ancient horses. In effect, selective and retro-breeding of superior game for a superior human race to hunt—a mania that stretched to the uprooting of indigenous Slav plants to make room for Aryan seed.

The firebombing of Dresden took place on February 13–14, 1944. February 14, 1944, was not only St. Valentine's Day, but was the seventh Wednesday before Easter and the first day of Lent—that is, *Ash Wednesday*, the day on which many Christians receive a mark of ashes on their foreheads as a token of penitence and mortality.

In Poland alone, 860,000 Jews were resettled, with 75,000 Germans taking over the acquired lands. 1,300,000 Poles were shipped to Germany as slave labor, with another 330,000 being simply shot. The invading Germans, remaining Poles, and Jews now stood in breadlines or, rather, three separate lines. Germans received 2,613 calories, Poles 669, Jews 184.

Soldiers are witnesses and there is a false belief that they should recover from what they have seen and done, and had done to them. Combat is so separate, so distant from normalcy that to expect soldiers to return easily from battle during or after war is an illusive prospect. All to say that much of what propels a soldier's worldview and living must stem from war-learned behavior—reliance on instinct and the ugly effectiveness of violence.

There's a passage where Paul Berlin is going to war and he looks at his own hands, "my hands, my hands." Love of one's limbs. Love of their presence, because in war there's always the proximate danger of their absence. No hands. No legs. No feet. No testicles. No head. That passage in Cacciato was written with a real purpose in mind: "my hands." Those are things we take for granted. We don't look at our hands and take a shower and say "my hands." But war teaches you to value those hands.—Tim O'Brien, qtd. in Herzog

There were three penises, two complete faces, which looked like masks they were so complete, five soles of feet, their hands, and few other parts. The largest body part was a section of a rib cage with parts of four rib bones connected to a small section of the shoulder.—Frederick Downs, writing about counting bodies, or parts of them, to sustain the American policy of attrition; qtd. in Nadelson

After counting, Downs's men situated one of the Viet Cong hands into the soft ground and stuck a cigarette between two Viet Cong fingers. "It looked great," Downs said.

Years after, veterans still find memories of combat victory and killing exhilarating. Soldiers as yet "uncooked" by combat often scrutinize the face and body of the killed enemy in wonder at their ability to create something as profound and enduring as death. Soldiers tie themselves to the dead by photographing dead enemy soldiers or by taking the possessions of the dead as trophies to preserve the moment.—Dr. Theodore Nadelson

One of Dr. Nadelson's patients puts it more crudely: "You could do anything you wanted—shit, I was eighteen—kill anyone or anything in Vietnam and get away with it. It was like being drunk and walking around with a hard-on."

. . . though as Nadelson points out: If soldiers "cannot be aroused to kill to avoid their own death and that of their comrades, they are a detriment to the safety of others."

Mission Accomplished.

Few things in this world are as unforgiving, pitiless, ungovernable, and irrecoverable as lead and steel loosed from a weapon. The transfigurations they effect on the bodies of friend and foe alike form a permanent backdrop to all of a soldier's future visions. While others experience intervals of silence between thoughts, a combat veteran's intervals will be filled with rubbery Halloween mask heads housing skulls shattered into tiny shards, schemeless mutilation, and shocked, pained expressions that violent and premature death casts on a dead face. These images are war's graffiti.—John Wolfe, qtd. in Anderson, When War Becomes Personal

First-World Problem:
Tanorexia, a term used to explain addiction to sunbathing or use of tanning beds.

Gandalf.

Because I'd served a few years as a church missionary before attending college, I was older than my college peers. What I failed to grasp when, in my panic, I contracted with the air force was that the draft lottery dates drawn applied to *that* year's (1970's) newly turned 19-year-old males. I turned 24 that summer and could have completed school and soon, especially with the war winding down, moved past the specified draft-age window (19-to-25-year-olds). I'd been born on July 9 all right, but July 9, *1946*, not *1951*. I joined the air force because I misinterpreted what the lottery meant for me.

I had joined the air force to avoid the walking tour of Southeast Asia, then spent the next 22 years in the service. In 1970, besides confusing the rules of the draft lottery, I also managed to select the single service then willing to commission colorblind officers—or, as the government puts it, color-vision-deficient persons.

I was commissioned an air force second lieutenant on July 14, 1971. One hundred eighty-two years to the day French peasants stormed the Bastille.

What the FBI Said:
Serial killers target Rest Stops.

Three Quick Writing Lessons:
WORDS NOT TO USE IN DIALOGUE—
She/he *chortled. Guffawed. Hissed. Uttered stentoriously.*

HOW NOT TO END A STORY—
He could see in his brother's bulging eye the reflection of the glowing mushroom cloud rising behind him.

THE STORY I'LL FAIL MY WRITERS FOR—
"Dwarf Rapes Nun, Escapes in UFO"

There is in short no absolute Time Standard.—Glenn D. Considine

A child-nurse by the name of Cindy waltzed into my hospital room the day following my colostomy. She wore a pink-striped smock and carried

a catalog of what she called "appliances." An appliance consisted of an adhesive flange and a plastic bag you could snap on to shit in. Cindy called the bags "pouches"—ostomy pouches.

Ostomy: general term for an operation in which an artificial opening is created for the elimination of bodily waste.

In her catalog, Cindy turned to the "Designer Pouches."

"*Designer?*"

"Yes, colored pouches—mauve, night-blue, amber—tiger pouches, elephant pouches..."

"Elephant?"

"Yes, elephant. And leopard." Cindy pointed out there were plain pouches too.

"I'm shopping for Tupperware," I said.

"Well, they are airtight," Cindy said. Then: "In the plain pouch line, you have transparent and opaque, and you have disposable and reuseable."

"Opaque and disposable. Buy those, Cindy. Sink my money into those."

My mother would pull the sock over a light bulb to darn it.

The women who caught my teenage eye were Angie Dickinson, Julie Christie, and Eva Marie Saint. The movies that caught my eye were *Rio Bravo*, *Doctor Zhivago*, and a low-budget Western entitled *Stalking Moon* in which Eva Marie depended on a young Gregory Peck.

My father and I grubbed out a basement beneath our house that already stood. We first dug a narrow dirt slope down to the depth we wanted, knocking away a section of the concrete foundation. My father shored up that span with joists and posts he termed studs.

The procedure was to dig by hand, dumping shovelfuls into a 55-gallon drum. The drum was then hoisted up the slope by means of a tripod made of poles that had been rigged with a cable and pulley. The system required two trucks, one to hoist the barrel and one to dump the barrel

into. It worked like this: Once the filled barrel was raised to the top of the tripod, the second truck was backed in, the barrel lowered, tipped, then hoisted by its bottom to empty the dirt. We hauled the dirt to the field where we fenced the cow.

Even at 14, I knew this was not the most efficient approach, but when I later worked in the mines, I learned that was where my father had gotten the idea. It was probably the same place he got the barrel and the cable and the pulley. Maybe even the poles. It took us a couple of summers—full summers—to complete the digging.

1959. On August 19, Butte miners walk out on strike. The work stoppage continues until February 11, 1960.

In my basement room I hung a punching bag that I used. I did my homework in my room and worked at quick-drawing my toy guns, though the pistols and their holsters looked real—cowhide and steel. I gave myself a name and official rank: Slade Chance, as in *Marshal* Slade Chance. I could work up tears over people I had to kill. I could work up an erection over the women I was meant to save or impress. I was 16.

No doubt my inspiration was Howard Hawks's 1959 treasure *Rio Bravo* in which John Wayne is Sheriff John T. Chance and Angie Dickinson is a dancehall gambler named Feathers.

> Feathers: *How does a . . . how does a man get to be a sheriff?*
> John T. Chance: *Gets lazy. Gets tired of selling his gun all over. Decides to sell it in one place.*
> Feathers: *I'd say you made a poor sale.*
> John T. Chance: *A lot of people around here'll agree with you.*
> Feathers: *But . . . it's still a sale and it's too late to back out.*

In 1959, Angie Dickinson was 28. When I first saw the film, I was 13. Ricky Nelson, who played Colorado Ryan, a gunslinger and singer, was but six years older and an established teenage idol. Forty-five when he died, Nelson was then the age of my father when I left home to live in France.

59

Feathers: *I thought you were never going to say it.*
John T. Chance: *Say what?*
Feathers: *That you love me.*
John T. Chance: *I said I'd arrest you.*
Feathers: *It means the same thing, you know that.*

In the 1970s, I was stationed in Alaska as part of the DEW line. Angie Dickinson showed up at the radar site in *Big Bad Mama*. She was 43, and in the film she disrobes, an original cougar.

One of the best-known exploitation films ever made, *Big Bad Mama* has been referred to as "one hell of a B-grade movie." Critic Christopher Null contends, ". . . you haven't lived until you've witnessed William Shatner sweating over Dickinson's naked body."

In those days of yore, before the Internet or DVDs, we received five reel-to-reel movies each week when the mail plane wasn't weathered out. Movies were screened twice a day, to accommodate both day and night shifts. At the end of five days, the most attended movie was shown again. *Big Bad Mama* was screened six times.

What the Doctor Said:
If you experience sudden loss of vision, stop using Cialis . . .

In six months of firebombing, starting with the Tokyo raid, civilian casualties in Japan doubled those suffered by the Japanese military worldwide in 45 months of war. By the time "Little Boy" and "Fat Man" struck, B-29s had triumphantly firebombed five-dozen Japanese cities.

Firebombing is efficient, as approximately 85 percent of the weight of a firebomb is fuel.

Carpal tunnel syndrome didn't exist until it became affordable. People used to have to work anyway.

1941. December 12. Word is received that LeRoy Carpenter is killed in action in the Philippines. LeRoy is Butte's first reported casualty.

Marine Corps Capt. Ronald Gregory Babich, 28, of 1704 McDonald Ave., was killed in the vicinity of Quang Tin, Vietnam, Friday (2 Jun 1967), the Defense Department announced Wednesday. Capt. Babich was gradu- ated from Butte High School and from the University of Montana in 1960, receiving a degree in forestry. He married Shannon Flynn in Butte, 21 Mar 1957.

Over 7 million tons of bombs were dropped by the United States during the Vietnam War, almost four times the total dropped in World War II.

. . . we were wrong, terribly wrong.—Robert McNamara, 20 years after the Fall of Saigon

An exterminating weapon of choice employed by Allied forces in their battles against the last-ditch resistance of the Japanese in the Pacific islands was the flame thrower. The portable version, carried on the backs of ground troops, had a range of 45 yards and enough fuel for 10 seconds of continuous fire. Larger units installed in tank turrets doubled the range and could carry enough fuel for a burst of up to 60 seconds. Because these instruments, portable or no, projected streams of oil burning at temperatures of 2000°F, mere seconds of use proved enough. They were especially effective against Japanese defending caves and coconut bunkers.

Because McNamara published his recollections of the Vietnam War the same week that the Alfred P. Murrah Federal Building was bombed, the former secretary of defense kept showing up on the screen between reports of casualties from Oklahoma City. In a *Harper's* essay, Lewis Lapham compares Robert McNamara to Timothy McVeigh in that both employed bombing as a means of rhetoric.

Two pages from its end—in a book of 335 pages—McNamara gets to this: *In the end we must confront the fate of those Americans who served in Vietnam and never returned.* Then in the painful dodge of *In Retro- spect*, the secretary continues: *Does the unwisdom of our intervention nullify their effort and loss? I think not. . . . That our effort in Vietnam proved unwise does not make their sacrifice any less noble.*

61

In Retrospect was a bestseller during the year that its author celebrated, in rosy health, his 79th year. The last photo in the book is one of the 79-year-old himself, atop a mountain with a pal. *While writing this manuscript,* McNamara begins his caption of the photo, *I took time off for a winter climb of Homestake Peak (13,200 feet) on the Continental Divide in Colorado.*

The average age of the Vietnam War dead was 23 years.

... there is something wrong with a culture in which McNamara is feted for his "guts" [for confessing] while George McGovern and Gene McCarthy who opposed McNamara's mistakes, are regarded as nobodies.
—Mickey Kaus

May we remember that in addition to our losses—200,000 wounded, 58,000 dead—the Vietnamese suffered up to 2 million wounded and 3 million dead.

In Afghanistan, Taliban clerics, as a matter of course, ordered amputations—a hand, a foot, combinations. A father of seven, picnicking near Kabul, was accused of spying. Unknown to the man, Taliban troops had been encamped nearby. Pulled from his home three days after and escorted to an unused soccer field, his left hand and his right foot were removed. His foot now missing below the ankle and his hand above the wrist, the 37-year-old man was not the only patient that day in Kabul to be sent home with stumps blunted by poorly stitched skin folds. Eyes wide, the man in the newspaper photo has a hunted expression.

A leading cause of amputation is land mines. By last count, over 250 million land mines (approximately one mine per able-bodied American) are thought to be stockpiled around the world, with some 70 million already deployed. Land mines are cheap, but defusing them is expensive. The cost ratio to mine versus to de-mine is 3:1000.

Should it be remembered that America's longest war—15 years—was for Vietnam, with its longer history, its shortest?

How to Write What Can't Be Written:
He says, "You've never seen anything
unless you've seen a man hit in the chest
with an RPG round."

I said, "I guess not," and drank on
into the heavy Asian night, weighted and packed.

I thought how many times you could say,
"You've never seen anything unless you've
seen . . ." and then go on, just fill in
the blanks . . .

> *an F-4 Phantom drop napalm along a tree line*

> *an illumination round light up the perimeter*
> *as night probes catch in the outer defenses*

> *body bags lined up at the edge of the pad,*
> *rotors rippling the plastic as they descend*

And I said, long after that night, after I'd felt their
names carved in that stone, "You've never seen anything . . .
anything . . . anything . . ."
—Dale Ritterbusch, "Conversation"

The AP reports on an 11-year-old with the Northern Alliance left to guard a wounded Taliban warrior outside Mazar-e-Sharif, the front advancing after days of insistent bombing. A British photojournalist caught the boy on film. The age of the Russian carbine makes the boy himself look old. The Brit later reported the boy had a ready response when asked what he thought should be done with the prisoner he'd been marooned to guard: "They should remove legs."

Like land mines, cluster bombs are cheap and effective and dangerous following approved or scheduled war. Designed to undo concentrated troop and tank formations, cluster bombs are dropped from planes in canisters that open at preset altitudes. In its turn, each canister releases up to 200 armor-piercing bomblets that drift to earth on parachutes. The bomblets are designed to explode upon contact. The thinnest part

of a tank is its top surface, in the way that a soldier's most vital spot is his covered or uncovered skull. Of course, not all bomblets explode and because they are delivered from altitude, weather conditions can cause unexpected and wide dispersal.

I suppose admitting mistakes is better than not admitting mistakes. But McNamara was a more sympathetic figure when he seemed tortured by guilt in private than now, when he is cashing in on it in public. There is something creepy, even slightly obscene, about the whole process, and it gets creepier upon inspection.—Mickey Kaus

Pentagon strategists privately acknowledge that, in Afghanistan, it was a mistake to make humanitarian-aid food rations dropped by the United States the same color and relative size as cluster bomblets. Bomblets that survive impact, even those penetrating earth, can be detonated by perching birds, passing cows, a farmer's plow—or the touch of a hand, maiming or killing anyone who would mistake these containers for food.

Entr'acte

During the fall of 1993, a Midwestern university-trained anesthesiologist undertook a hike in the Rockies. In an unexpected turn, a boulder he rested against toppled to break his leg and to pin him to the earth. Unable to shift the stone, he said he thought of coyotes and wolverines and traps and bears. The doctor said later that he'd thought also of wild hogs and snakes, though he said he knew at the time that hogs were not native to the region and that snakes were in hibernation. "I wasn't myself," he explained.

Snow in the forecast, temperature and darkness falling, he determined to amputate his leg. Constructing a tourniquet of his shirt, the doctor then unfolded a fishing knife he'd sharpened the day before on a two-stage electric sharpener he'd ordered from Chef's Choice. He flayed the skin and fat to expose the left and then the right side of his knee joint. He parted tendons and ligaments, blood vessels, and nerves. He would work, he said, then pause to gather himself. He severed the

patellar ligament to separate the femur and tibia, then pulled the thigh-bone free. He dragged himself to reach his F250 Super Duty Ford 4WD.

It was a standard transmission he manipulated to the nearest town. U.S. Weather Service satellite photos confirmed a less than predicted storm—a light but wet snow—blanketed the area the following day. In this way, the doctor forgives himself for having removed his leg.—from "Stumps"

By his own admission in his memoir, McNamara notes that, as early as 1965, he thought the war impossible to win, and that by 1966 he had told reporters (off the record) that massive bombing would not force North Vietnam to end the war. By 1967, he believed the United States would suffer a major national disaster if it did not withdraw from Southeast Asia. Nonetheless McNamara said nothing in public to stop a war that was to continue another bloody seven years.

McNamara cast his silence as allegiance to his president, Lyndon John-son. He even claimed that as the departing secretary of defense "[his] voice wouldn't have made any difference."

Unelected officials should not steal their President's mandate to pursue an independent course. But a thousand dead Americans a month create their own constituency. Even military discipline admits a higher duty than hierarchical loyalty when power is badly used and puts lives at risk.—Max Frankel

How to Explain What Soldiers Know:
I was always embarrassed by the words sacred, glorious, and sacrifice and the expression in vain. We had heard them, sometimes standing in the rain almost out of earshot, so that only the shouted words came through, and had read them, on proclamations that were slapped up by billposters over other proclamations, now for a long time, and I had seen nothing sacred, and the things that were glorious had no glory and the sacrifices were like the stockyards at Chicago if nothing was done with the meat except to bury it. . . . Abstract words such as glory, honor, courage,

or hallow were obscene beside the concrete names of rivers, the numbers
of regiments and the dates.—Ernest Hemingway

In 1598, Spanish explorer Don Juan de Onate conquered New Mexico. For 220 years México Nuevo belonged to Spain, passing to Mexico and then on to the United States. When the people of Acoma Pueblo battled the Spanish, killing Juan de Zaldivar—Onate's nephew and field marshal—the governor condemned 24 Acoma to the amputation of a foot. It is also claimed that Onate banished the one-footed men's wives and children into slavery, dragging them from the wounded men and the pile of feet.

It is estimated that the 1991 Persian Gulf War itself accounts for 1.2 million unaccounted-for cluster bomblets.

In 1998, New Mexico commemorated the 400-year-old Spanish settlement of the state. Prior to the celebration, a larger-than-life statue of Onate was commissioned and a visitor center established in Alcalde, New Mexico. On January 6, 1998, a lone dissident, or some number of Indian commandos, sliced off the right foot of the tall bronze man. It has been determined that the vandal or vandals, under cover of darkness, expertly applied a power grinder.

"Persistence of Vision" is a scientific term for the human ability to see an object long after the object has been removed.

There is little evidence among Germans of widespread refusal to co-operate with the Nazis. Beyond this, the British Foreign Office and the U.S. State Department turned down rescue plans that would have saved numbers of Jews from the furnaces. A large number of the murdered European Jews were burned.

The practice of cremation on open fires was introduced at least as early as 1000 B.C. The *Iliad* refers to the royal cremation of the hero Hector. Hector was incinerated following 17 days of lavish mourning. Cremation in Europe became rare, however, except during emergencies

such as plague years. In 1656, for instance, 60,000 plague victims were burned in Naples in a single week. Modern cremation has evolved beyond open fires. Bodies are placed in chambers where concentrated heat transforms them in 60 minutes to a few pounds of powder.

So marijuana is illegal, but it's okay to drop napalm on gooks?
—W. D. Ehrhart

Oswiecim, better known by its German name, Auschwitz—or, more properly, Auschwitz-Birkenau—is a small town in southern Poland. Established in 1940, the camp was, for five years, a model of efficient work. At its peak, the death camp's *Badeanstalten* ("bathhouses") accommodated 2,000 people at once. Twelve thousand inmates could be processed per day. With its numerous and orderly prison blocks, gas chambers, and crematoria, Oswiecim covered but 15 square miles, though 2 million or so people were there housed and exterminated. Once murdered, the method of the disposal of Jews was fire. Generally, the inmates were worked to death or starved, though qualified Nazi doctors performed medical experiments on a select few.

There were, remarkably, 2.7 million U.S. participants in the Vietnam War, in a strip of a nation you could drive the length of on a good highway in 10 hours, the width of in three.

They could have sent me to prison, Mom. To prison. For smoking pot. You know what it says on the back of my Purple Heart Medal? "For Military Merit." I'm guilty, all right. I'm guilty of murder, of attempted murder, arson, assault and battery, aggravated assault, assault with a deadly weapon, robbery, burglary, larceny, disorderly conduct, you name it, I've done it. And according to our so-called system, it was all perfectly legal. They gave me a medal for it. Am I relieved about the way the trial turned out. Yes. Am I happy about it? Not hardly.—W. D. Ehrhart, following his acquittal from a drug charge

Without knowing the depth or scope of what psychic and spiritual damage lies spidered within a number like 2.7 million, we do know

that more than 200,000 U.S. soldiers were wounded in Vietnam—and we know, too, that 33,000 of these persons are permanently paralyzed, para- or quadriplegic.

In the long haul of history, a stone ax crushing a skull is no different from a Tomahawk missile, except in its efficiency . . .

The total mass of the fragments of a split atom is usually less than the combined mass of the original nucleus and the bombarding neutron. The missing mass, m, is transformed into energy, E, in accordance with Einstein's equation $E=mc^2$, where c is the velocity of light. Because the velocity of light is so large (186,000 miles per second), a small amount of mass corresponds to an enormous amount of energy. This explains the small size but large effects of atomic bombs.

The amount of energy released in the process of fission is so great that the complete fission of 1.5 pounds of uranium or plutonium would create the equivalent of the explosive energy of 24 million pounds of TNT. One characteristic of the atomic bomb is the high temperature it spawns. The maximum temperature at the bursting point reaches several million degrees. The energy of thermal radiation is about 35 percent of the whole energy of the bomb. An enormous amount of energy, about 7×10^{12} calories, is, therefore, released as thermal radiation from a standard atomic bomb. Thermal radiation affects flesh.

Then there is Cynthia Ozick's short story "The Shawl," a strafing account of a death-camp murder of a stick-limbed child. Though born in time to have been interned in a death camp, Cynthia Ozick wasn't; she was, at the story's fictional time, a cheerleader in high school in New Jersey.

When you have done your best, it doesn't matter how good it is. That is for others to say. . . . An act of the imagination is an act of self-acceptance. . . . Writing is a way of saying you and the world have a chance.
—Richard Hugo

By way of vindication and excuse, it has been pointed out that the

horrifying atomic bomb death toll in Hiroshima was in fact somewhat less than that occasioned five months before by the patterned dropping of ordinary incendiary bombs on Tokyo. In a single night, one-fourth of the city was torched, 1 million made homeless, and over 80,000 citizens were burned. The core temperature of Tokyo ranged from 1000° to 2000°F. Water in the city's canals boiled.

How to Write about Race:

1942: New York

The Red Cross Doesn't Accept Black Blood

U.S. soldiers embark for the war fronts. Many are black under the command of white officers.

Those who survive will return home. The blacks will enter by the back door, and, in the Southern states, continue to live, work, and die apart, and even then will lie in separate graves. Hooded Ku Klux Klansmen will still insure that blacks do not intrude into the white world, and above all into the beds of white women.

The war accepts blacks, thousands and thousands of them, but not the Red Cross. The Red Cross bans black blood in the plasma banks, so as to avoid the possibility that races might mix by transfusion.

The research of Charles Drew, inventor of life, has finally made it possible to save blood. Thanks to him, plasma banks are reviving thousands of dying men on the battlefields of Europe.

When the Red Cross decides to reject the blood of blacks, Drew, director of the Red Cross plasma service, resigns. Drew is black.

—Eduardo Galeano

I know two people who have backed their cars through closed garage doors. One young, one old. Both shocked.

2010. The average American eats 200 pounds of meat annually, an increase of 50 pounds per person from 50 years ago.

Producing animal protein requires eight times the amount of fossil fuel as producing the comparable amount of plant protein. Going meatless two days a week saves the same amount of fuel that can be accomplished by switching from a standard sedan to a hybrid.

2010. By most counts, British Petroleum lost at least 30,000 barrels of oil a day into the Gulf waters. A barrel is 42 gallons, so 30,000 barrels would equate to nearly 1.3 million gallons a day. As compared to the Exxon Valdez disaster in 1989 that spilled 10.8 million gallons of oil into Prince William Sound.

Every 10 days Exxon Valdez all over again . . .

The plastic bags Americans use require, annually, 12 million barrels of oil.

Seventeen million barrels of oil are consumed each year to produce plastic water bottles for American use, and this in a country where clean tap water is ubiquitous . . .

Why we go for cheap oil was explained to me by pointing out that the daily loss of oil from the BP spill in the Gulf would power all the cars in Texas for two minutes.

What is it that the United States believes it can do in Afghanistan that proved unavailable to Alexander the Great, Genghis Khan, the Brits, and the Soviet Union all during their heydays?

The artist Christo and his wife wrapped a Paris bridge and a Berlin building with fabric, curtained a Colorado valley, encircled Florida islands, gated New York City's Central Park . . .

Over the River is a two-week temporary work of Christo art that calls for 5.9 miles of silvery fabric to be suspended above the Arkansas River, spaced along a 40-mile stretch of the river between Salida and Cañon City in south-central Colorado.

Cotopaxi, Colorado is an Arkansas River town (pop. 3000) known for its whitewater rafting, and now for being the midway point of Christo's drapings.

Linda M. is known for her sandwiches at the deli counter of the Coto-paxi Store, and now for her reaction to Christo's plan: *Sheets across the river, that's not art. Now wolves. Wolves are art. I like wolves. I have wolf pictures, wolf puzzles, wolf drinking glasses, wolf plates. Anything with wolves on it. My husband said if I buy one more thing with wolves on it, he's going to divorce me. And then at Christmas he buys me something with wolves on it. But hanging sheets across the river . . .*

I encountered an art installation on the entry steps of a museum in Utah. It was July, and randomly placed on the granite steps were blocks of ice that were melting. Piled atop the blocks were dead tree leaves, oak and maple.

How to Write about Torture:

1970: Montevideo

Portrait of a Torture Trainer

The Tupamaro guerrillas execute Dan Anthony Mitrione, one of the North American instructors of the Uruguayan police.

The dead man gave his courses to officers in a soundproof base-ment. For his practical lessons he used beggars and prostitutes pulled off the street. He showed his pupils the effects of various electric volt-ages on the most sensitive parts of the human body, and how to apply emetics and other chemical substances efficaciously. In recent months three men and a woman died during these classes in the Technique of Interrogation.

Mitrione despised disorder and dirt. A torture chamber should be as aseptic as an operating room. And he detested incorrect language: "Not balls, commissioner. *Testicles.*"

He also abominated useless expense, unnecessary movement, avoid-able damage.

"It's an art more than a technique," he said. "*The precise pain, in the precise place, in the precise amount.*"—Eduardo Galeano

With *Over the River*, Christo must go it alone, as his bushy red-headed wife Jeanne-Claude has died.

71

Within an hour of the first firestorm (the RAF raid on Hamburg, Germany, July 28, 1943), the Hamburg Fire Department recorded the incident by coining the word *Feuersturm* to describe it.

When many buildings are ablaze, great heat is generated and the convection that the fires cause not only sucks in air but disseminates sparks and burning debris to start other conflagrations. The more fires, the greater the heat and convection until, in seconds, all fires coalesce. Hurricane winds are then created, ingesting oxygen and promoting temperatures. At 2000°F, blood boils.

SAVAK: a contraction of Farsi words for the security and information organization under the reign of the Shah. Following the ascension of the Islamic republic, a SAVAK official appears on Western TV. On screen, the official's face is distorted, voice warped: "Many of us will have problems making ends meet."

Instead of getting married again, I'm going to find a woman I don't like and give her a house.—Lewis Grizzard

Entr'acte
1979. My first semester as a college instructor. Three years before, I'd come across Robert Penn Warren's poem "Waiting" in the *Atlantic*. I remember because I fell into the well of the poem. As a diligent student I felt I could write an essay about the abstractions of Warren's poem—love, Nature, disease, death: conditions of life over which we have little, if any, control—but I felt, too, I wouldn't have thought to write:

> *You will have to wait. Until it. Until*
> *The last owl hoot has quavered to a*
>
> *Vibrant silence and you realize there is no breathing*
> *Beside you, and dark curdles toward dawn. Until*
>
> *Drought breaks, too late to save the corn,*
> *But not too late for flood, and the dog-fox, stranded*

On a sudden islet, barks in hysteria in the alder-break. Until
The doctor enters the waiting room, and

His expression betrays all, and you wish
He'd take his God-damned hand off your shoulder. Until

The woman you have lived with all the years
Says, without rancor, that life is the way life is, and she

Had never loved you, had believed the lie
 only for the sake of the children.

For one thing, would I have thought of the word *curdle*? And would I
have thought of the particulars: the stranded dog-fox, the doctor and
the hand on my shoulder, the wife who hadn't loved me, the vibrant,
quavering hoot? These citings of some of what we hold loose rein over,
and what we concoct to pretend control.

 . . . Until
You become uncertain of French irregular verbs,

And by a strange coincidence begin to take Catholic instruction from
Monsignor O'Malley, who chews a hangnail. Until

You realize, truly, that our Saviour died for us all,
And as tears gather in your eyes, you burst out laughing,

For the joke is certainly on Him, considering
What we are.

Then the swivel, the essential swerve of the poem:

 . . . Until

You pick the last alibi off, like a scab, and
Admire the inwardness as beautiful as inflamed flesh

Or summer sunrise. Until you
Remember, surprisingly, that common men have done good deeds. Until it

Grows on you that, at least, God
Has allowed us the grandeur of certain utterances.

In 1976, when I read Warren's poem, I was 30. I felt, as I say, I could have written then an essay about my lack of control over death, love, disease, wildfire, nuclear fusion, whatnot. I believed, too, I possessed sufficient proof that no act of will or imposition of structure or thought could fix the fact and risk of being human. I had not, however, put this news to myself in quite Red Warren's way. I felt jealous.

Barroom Graffito:
JESUS Loves You. Every One Else Thinks You're An Asshole

Cremation has returned to fashion. Many Protestant churches actively support cremation as a principal form of burial. The Roman Catholic Church has lifted its prohibition. The Jewish religion continues to forbid it.

If it seems to fall to the historian to make distinctions among wars, each war's larger means and ends, the trajectory for the artist, regardless of culture or time, seems to fall toward an individual's disillusionment, the means and ends of war played out in the personal. For the individual soldier, the sweeping facts of history are accurately written not in the omniscient, third-person plural, but in the singular first.

W. H. Auden, who came into his fullness as a poet as fascism was creeping across Europe, wrote about that scourge and then concluded that "poetry makes nothing happen," that nothing he ever wrote saved one Jew from the gas chambers. Yet, art markets authority. Why else would officials at the United Nations have decided to cover the tapestry of Picasso's *Guernica*, as council members met to discuss the start of Gulf War II?

War is hell, but that's not the half of it, because war is also mystery and terror and adventure and courage and discovery and holiness and pity and despair and longing and love. War is nasty; war is fun. War is thrilling; war is drudgery. War makes you a man; war makes you dead.
—Tim O'Brien

That scrap of history we call our lives . . .

In Saudi Arabia, your right hand can be amputated for theft, but for highway robbery, your left foot is removed.

To delight in war is a merit in the soldier, a dangerous quality in the captain, and a positive crime in the statesman.—George Santayana

Amputate: From the Latin *amputāre—am* "around" + *putāre* "to trim, prune."

Employing the daily BP spill in the Gulf, I could drive my SUV a third of the way to the sun: six days of oil for the roundtrip, though, at 80 mph, it would require 160 years or so.

War hath no fury like a noncombatant.—C. E. Montague

Is my math right?

The advent of cell phones has forced millions of people sitting in restaurants, reading on commuter trains, idling in waiting rooms, attending the theatre to become party to the most intimate details of other people's lives—their breakups, the health of their portfolios, their psychotherapeutic progress, their arguments with their bosses or boyfriends or parents. This experience of being constantly exposed to other people's life stories is matched only by the inexhaustible eagerness of people to tell their life stories . . .—Daniel Mendelsohn

The first time I encountered someone with a cell phone "hands-free" device was in an Albertson's grocery store. The woman walked the aisles in front of me, speaking German. I thought she was demented. She was on the phone.

Flying first class is the only time, since childhood, that someone has poured milk on to my cereal.

I was surprised to see the Sarah Palin sticker on the 30-year-old VW bus.

. . . writers simply do what human beings have always done. They write

stories because they have to; because they cannot rest until they have tried as hard as they can to write the stories. They cannot rest because they are human, and all of us need to speak into the silence of mortality, to interrupt and ever so briefly stop that quiet flow, and with stories try to understand at least some of it.—Andre Dubus

I don't think the workshops taught me too much about craft, but they did teach me about the importance of making things, not just reading things. You care about things that you make, and that makes it easier to care about things that other people make.—Louis Menand

Ink runs from the corners of my mouth.
There is no happiness like mine.
I have been eating poetry.
—Mark Strand, from "Eating Poetry"

Friends don't let friends read junk.
—ad campaign for *North American Review*

My 10-year-old grandson demonstrated how to make a photo of the person calling appear when your cell phone rings. I started to tell him about the Sunday comics when I was his age. He has no idea who Dick Tracy is. "Dick Tracy?" he says.

Flash Gordon.

The same grandson (in first grade) was asked what three items he would carry aboard the *Mayflower*. He would carry, he said, deodorant, a flashlight, and a net—the net being for trapping turkeys.

As much as possible, I travel, locally and about, sans ID. If I die, shouldn't it be inconvenient for someone?

Madoff, Bernard.

Sabot, the French word for wooden shoe, appears as a word in English as early as 1607. According to the OED, it then meant in English what

it meant in French: A shoe made from a single piece of wood, shaped and hollowed out to fit the foot.

Sabotage debuted as a word associated with workers throwing wooden shoes into machines with intent to damage the machines. The first instances of *sabotage* were likely, then, peasant revolts against oppressive landowners and the emergence of mechanized harvesting tools.

In the *American Heritage Dictionary*, *sabotage* is found on the same page, in the same column, as *saber-toothed tiger* and *SAC,* the acronym of the Strategic Air Command, the step-brainchild of Gen. Curtis E. LeMay. Long before he hooked up with George C. Wallace as the vice-presidential candidate on the 1968 American Independent third-party *Bomb-'em-back-to-the-Stone-Age* ticket, LeMay (in 1945, the youngest major-general in the Army Air Corps) took over the 21st Bomber Command in the Mariana Islands.

Robert McNamara, as a subordinate, was an aide to General LeMay during the firebombing of Japan.

I was on the island of Guam in his command in March 1945. In that single night, we burned to death one hundred thousand Japanese civilians in Tokyo. Men, women and children. . . . I was part of a mechanism that, in a sense, recommended it. . . . LeMay said if we lost the war that we would have all been prosecuted as war criminals. And I think he's right. He . . . and I'd say I . . . were behaving as war criminals.

Later, McNamara, as secretary of defense, fired LeMay from his position of chief of staff of the air force, as he believed that LeMay was dangerously bomb-happy, a notion congealed in Stanley Kubrick's satisfying caricature of LeMay in *Dr. Strangelove.*

General Jack D. Ripper.

It's true LeMay argued with John Kennedy about the need to bomb Cuba.

Sterling Hayden, who starred as Ripper, had served as a marine and an

undercover agent with the OSS. He ran guns to Yugoslavian partisans and parachuted into action in the Balkans, winning a Silver Star for gallantry. He was, after the war, briefly, a member of the Communist Party who then cooperated with the House Un-American Activities Committee. In his biography, Hayden expressed contempt for himself.

LeMay inaugurated the low-level bombing tactics that burned 59 Japanese cities. The tightly packed wooden cities of Japan proved incendiaries effective.

Gen. Thomas "Tommy" Power, who flew the lead aircraft into Tokyo: *It was the greatest single disaster incurred by any enemy in military history. It was greater than the combined damage of Hiroshima and Nagasaki. There were more casualties than in any other military action in the history of the world.*

Tokyo was struck twice. A total of 1,022 aircraft dropped some 7,000 tons of bombs. With 50.8 percent of the city reduced to ashes, Tokyo was removed from the list of incendiary targets.

To be fair, 1945 was a year of excessive rainfall and floods in Japan. In some cases, earthquakes destroyed homes, but by the end of five months of firebombing, a quarter of the houses in Japan were gone. Put another way, 22 million people were homeless.

As a captain and protocol officer at Headquarters Strategic Air Command, I once escorted Curtis LeMay through its hallowed halls.

SAC Headquarters was the castle LeMay had built, but by the time I walked beside him, he was an old man in a shabby suit and stone deaf in his left ear.

Rule: Trail a senior officer, one step back, to his left.

The Japanese word for *iris* is the same as the word for *bravery*, which is the same as the word for *victory*. Ancient Japanese warrior armor is covered with the images of flowers.

Sakura (cherry blossoms) were esteemed because they fall at the height of their beauty, thus signifying samurai grace and resignation in the face of death.

The state flower of Alaska is a discarded and rusted 55-gallon drum.

When stationed for the air force in the Brooks Range in central Alaska, I experienced weather that dipped to more than -60°F.

As Napoleon's soldiers found out during the 1812 catastrophic eastern front, warming frozen limbs at open fires was as detrimental as their alternate method of rubbing snow on the affected parts. What you need are painkillers and water heated to 104–107 degrees. Then what you need is rehydration, a high-protein diet, and a course of antibiotics. This approach was not available at Stalingrad, or in the Ardennes, or in Korea either.

In his memoir, *Mission with LeMay*, it is clear that the general felt slighted in that he was never privileged to employ a nuclear bomb.

Uranium, plutonium; "Little Boy, Fat Man": the world knows those weapons now, every school child knows. No use describing the mushroom-shaped column, the unbelievable light, and weird color of the flash and resulting clouds . . . unearthly debris and steaming destruction and massive death. It's an old and familiar story now, from Bikini on. These bombs brought into the world not only their own speed and extent of desolation. They brought a strange pervading fear which does not seem to have affected mankind previously, from any other source. This unmitigated terror has no justice, no basis in fact. Nothing new about death, nothing new about deaths caused militarily. We scorched and boiled and baked to death more people in Tokyo on that night of March 9–10 than went up in vapor at Hiroshima and Nagasaki combined.

Curt was forced to satisfy his cravings with mere fire.

After Nagoya and Osaka, LeMay concluded *that the Toyko raid had not been a fluke.* Following the initial 10 days of firebombing, General

LeMay thought *that a man might have the right to some sort of mild celebration*. He sends for cigars. *I craved a celebration, and I was going to celebrate with Havanas or know the reason why.*

He could hardly wait to light up.

And: *I have indeed bombed a number of specific targets. They were military targets on which the attack was, in my opinion, justified morally. I've tried to stay away from hospitals, prison camps, orphan asylums, nunneries and dog kennels. I have sought to slaughter as few civilians as possible.*

Humans—despite their artistic pretensions, their sophistication, and their many accomplishments—owe their existence to a six-inch layer of topsoil and the fact that it rains.

The arts and humanities are not mere entertainment, to be turned to for relaxation after a busy day of solving differential equations; they are templates for living, for governing ourselves and our societies. Nor can science offer any help with the knottier problems besetting the human race. It can remedy bad smells, bad pains, and bad roads, but not bad behavior, bad government, or bad ideas.—John Derbyshire

LeMay couldn't smile. A botched sinus operation prevented him from curving his lips.

As suggested by a survey of a number of modern dictionaries, *sabotage* means interference with production, work, etc., undermining a cause, etc., injuring or attacking, instilling terror, etc. Consider a definition (number 3, say) for *saboteur*: 3. LeMay, Curtis E. (Emerson). See Japan, 1945.

Because it made marines feel dumb, the corps changed the term *booby trap* to *surprise firing devices.*

Euphemisms:
You think *friendly fire* isn't a powerful concept?

Entr'acte

Shah Muhammad Reza Pahlavi's father, Reza Khan, is an iron man. Reza Khan—*King of Kings, Shadow of the Almighty, Light of the Aryans, God's Vicar, Center of the Universe,* and *Commander-in-Chief*—builds roads, railways, airports, factories, schools, banks. His army herds nomads to the cities, levels mosques, imprisons or murders priests (the mullahs), strips women in the streets. Crowds are thinned and dispersed with bullets. The army is well-fed. People disappear. Shah Muhammad Reza Pahlavi inherits his father's generals, but not his father's height. Reza Pahlavi, early, sports elevator shoes, orders slaughters from the palace. The generals kneel before the son, kiss the shoes. In a land of flowing oil, Pahlavi's subjects collect cow dung to dry for fuel. Pahlavi's first wife, Fawzia, bathes daily in sweetened milk.

Reza Pahlavi, new Lord of Energy to the West, erects monuments of himself, vows creation of a second America founded on petroleum, poly-religion, concrete, plastic. Reza Pahlavi stands for photo ops for reporters. In public, he models European suits. On some level, based on these photos and selected quotes, the West forwards enthusiastic bribes, advisors, guns. A king's vanity, we learn, is different from our own. He has, among his king things, an armed army at hand.

In his turn, Reza Pahlavi releases his army into the streets. The army is well-fed. Hooded students, in European airports, pass pamphlets to hurried crowds. In Paris, at Orly airport, a group of students remove their shirts, their shoes. They display flayed backs, charred toes. One has no eyelids. (Were you to ask, he might explain he'd clamped his eyes against the torture of friends and that his closed lids had been burned away with lighted cigarettes.) At night, the students hobble to gather pamphlets from Orly's floors.

In Persia, death is followed by 40 days of mourning. It is believed that on the 40th day mourners can pronounce the names of killers, and that at that moment of pronouncement murderers will shudder in their shoes. "Death to the Shah" becomes the rhythm of Iran at intervals of 40 days.

Shah Muhammad Reza Pahlavi weeps when he flees Teheran. He explains to the Western press he has less money than people think. From the Shah's residence in St. Moritz, a courtier points, for French TV, to a photo in an old copy of *Paris Match*. The photo is a close-up of

81

the Shah's second infertile queen, Soraya Esfandiari, who in a lift line with others waits, democratically, to ski.

The expelled Reza Pahlavi roams, searches for a home. In disbelief, he dies barefooted in an unowned bed. For the news, the thin-boned Farah, the last of Pahlavi's wives, stands in Egypt, regally facing East, the whirring cameras. Her eyes crouch.

The state funeral in Cairo is almost private. Lionheartedly, Sadat welcomes two haggard kings, Nixon and Constantine of Greece. The three of them bury the Shah. Shortly, it is noted, rich Persians pop up in France and Beverly Hills.

Meantime, Islamic holy men squabble in medieval Persian streets eyeing house-sized portraits of the Awaited One—*Khomeini*—he who disappeared in the ninth century to now return to deliver his faithful from misery and the trod of kings. Afterward comes the End of the World. In evidence, royal tanks park in streets, untended. Crowds gather and part at will. Loudspeakers sprout like plants. Women dress from head to foot. But then: in Qom, Teheran, Tabriz, Meshed, Isfahan—under the hand of the Charitable and Merciful One—people begin to disappear.—from "The Peacock Throne," *Fire Road*

The Iranians "employed" 12-year-olds to fling themselves against barbed wire or to march, unarmed, into Iraqi mine fields in the face of machine-gun fire. The weaponless boys' ticket to paradise is a blood-red headband and a small metal key they wear into battle. The headbands are stenciled in Farsi: *Sar Allah*. So identified as divinely designated martyrs, the male children intend to use their keys to enter directly into heaven if killed in the holy war against Iraq. Rounded up by the clergy, indoctrinated in the Shiite tradition of martyrdom, and bowing to the Ayatollah Ruhollah Khomeini's will, the backs of their khaki-colored shirts declare: "I have the special permission of the Imam to enter heaven." As members of human-wave assaults, tens of thousands of such children have died. For the purpose of assured salvation, few pass puberty. An officer explains: "We have so few tanks."—Ibid.

In Iran, for promiscuous sex, accused men and women are hooded, then buried chest-deep in sand. A presiding judge will cast the first

stone, after which others may join in, selecting and throwing from a pile of apple-size rocks.

Sakineh Mohammadi Ashtiani.

It takes 15 minutes of stoning to kill people.

American families know the awful emptiness left by the young man who goes off to war and does not come home; but American families have been spared the knowledge of the destroyed home, with the children dead in it. War happens someplace else, far away. Farther away than ever before, in South Vietnam, a war is being waged in our name, the collective, anonymous name of the American people. And American weapons are killing and wounding uncounted Vietnamese children. Not 10 or 20 children, which would be tragedy enough, but hundreds killed and many more hundreds wounded every month. This terrible fact is officially ignored; no Government agency keeps statistics on the civilians of all ages, from babies to the very old, killed and wounded in South Vietnam. I have witnessed modern war in nine countries, but I have never seen a war like the one in South Vietnam.—Martha Gellhorn

Entr'acte

Driving from Denver, I'm boxed in on the interstate. To my front is half a long mobile home; to my left a brand-new concrete-gray cement truck, barreling south. Pulling to my rear and filling my own truck's mirror is a GMC four-wheel-drive from Texas. Its interior is wedged with hunters. I count them: six. There is some sort of rigged rifle rack behind the second seat, and I spot sleeping bags and piled gear, and what look to be tents, or parachutes. Two deer are strapped to the roof that gives with the weight. The men sport three-day beards, flannel shirts, and blaze-orange vests. Each of the shirts is a version of red. Dome lights on—maybe even a Coleman lantern—the faces seem both front- and back-lit, like a 40s flick. Somebody is smoking. Two of the men wear hats. The dead deer are strapped with white rope.

The trigger finger of my right hand throbs. There is, I see, blood clotted beneath the cuticle. The hunters flash their lights, but no exit is at

hand, my front and left still blocked by a cement truck and someone's severed home. The hunters flourish Colorado beer cans, wave at me to move. Unable to not, I check for weapons, peer for six. The roofed deer do not budge. The one to my mirror left rests formally on his side, the other more nearly on his back, forelegs bent and up, head turned, exposing a hollowed gut.

Again the hunters flash their lights, kiss my bumper. I edge to the right, work the narrow shoulder, and the hunters swerve, saluting as they pass. The passenger windows are mottled with blood—the deer gutted but not hung? In tow is a low-slung trailer, stacked with four more bucks and what my father pronounced "tarpauling." One buck's legs have been chopped or sawed off.

I roll to a stop to draw a breath. Five feet in front the sign: NO PARKING EMERGENCY ONLY. Despite the warning I perch on the shoulder. I wait for Texas to roll closer to Texas, and for the home and the truck to establish their positions. Why does it seem a stretch to think of a cement truck as new and of a house as perfectly divided? I ease back into traffic, the skin of the shoulder ice cracking. Once, I was helping my father split wood, and in steadying the steel wedge for him, had my hand smashed, when the wedge sprang sideways. The tips of my fingers ballooned and my nails turned blue and purple, the color of pulped things. With his right thumb my father struck a wooden match to heat a straightened paper clip he then pressed through my nails until each finger's pooled blood erupted: geysers. He then re-gloved my hand and we finished our work. When we stacked the wood, I worked as though my hands were burned. The heated clip had pierced my nails as though they were wax. How was it he was carrying paper clips and matches?

Cars blow by. Considering the road and the weather, it makes sense to drive below the limit. Near Larkspur, I depart the interstate to drive a parallel frontage road. It is a cloudless and full-moon night, and with the snow and no traffic, I can drive without lights. Lowering my window, I crane for the sound of unequal war, faint and persistent from the hills.—"Legal Limit"

Memory believes before knowing remembers.—William Faulkner

. . . this is a book of memory, and memory has its own story to tell. But I have done my best to make it a truthful story.—Tobias Wolff, from the epigraph for *This Boy's Life*

What to Engrave on Your Tomb:
I told you I was sick

Abu Ghraib was run by a female army reserve brigadier general. She had no experience running a prison and neither did most of the 3400 army reservists who worked for her. Prior to the American takeover of the facility, it had been known for its torture, executions, and otherwise vile conditions. As many as 50,000 prisoners were incarcerated at any one time during Saddam's reign. The coalition cleaned and repaired the prison, and installed toilets, showers, and a medical center.

Fast Facts:
Nine army reservists have been convicted of abusing detainees at the Abu Ghraib prison in Iraq:

Pfc. Lynndie England, a 22-year-old reservist from Fort Ashby, WV, was sentenced to three years in prison after being convicted on six of seven counts related to detainee abuse. England was found guilty of one count of conspiracy, four counts of maltreating detainees, and one count of committing an indecent act. She was acquitted on one conspiracy count.

Former Cpl. Charles Graner Jr., of Uniontown, PA, is serving a 10-year prison term at Fort Leavenworth. Prosecutors described Graner, who England has said is the father of her infant son, as the ringleader of a group of Abu Ghraib guards who mistreated Iraqis.

Former Spc. Megan Ambuhl, of Centreville, VA, a former Abu Ghraib guard now married to Graner, pleaded guilty in November 2004 to failing to prevent or report maltreatment of prisoners. She was discharged from the army without prison time.

Former Spc. Sabrina Harman, of Lorton, VA, was found guilty of conspiracy, maltreating detainees, and dereliction of duty. She was

sentenced to six months in prison after testimony about her acts of kindness toward Iraqis before she became an Abu Ghraib guard.

Former S. Sgt. Ivan Frederick of Buckingham, VA, was sentenced to eight and one-half years after pleading guilty to conspiracy, dereliction of duty, maltreatment of detainees, and other charges. Frederick said he helped place wires on a detainee's hands and told the prisoner he would be electrocuted if he fell while standing on a box.

Former Spc. Jeremy Sivits of Hyndman, PA, pleaded guilty to four counts for taking pictures of naked Iraqi prisoners being humiliated, including some of the photographs that triggered the Abu Ghraib scandal. He was sentenced to one year in prison.

Former Spc. Roman Krol, of Randolph, MA, admitted pouring water on naked detainees and forcing them to crawl around the floor. He also said he threw a foam football at them while they were handcuffed. Krol, who served in a military intelligence unit, was sentenced to 10 months in prison.

Former Spc. Armin Cruz, of Plano, TX, pleaded guilty to conspiracy and mistreating prisoners and was sentenced to eight months in prison. Cruz was part of the same military intelligence unit as Krol.

Former Sgt. Javal Davis, Roselle, NJ, was sentenced to six months in prison after pleading guilty to assault, dereliction of duty, and lying to army investigators. The former sergeant admitted stepping on the hands and feet of handcuffed detainees, and falling with his full weight on top of them.

The general who commanded the prison was relieved of duty, but not brought to trial, the indignity of rebuke considered sufficient.

From the Testimony of Lt. William L. Calley:
Q: Did you have a chance to look and observe what was in the ditch?
A: Yes, sir.
Q: What did you see?
A: Dead people, sir.
Q: Did you at any time direct anybody to push people in the ditch?
A: Like I said, sir, I gave the order to take those people through the ditch and had also told Meadlo if he couldn't move them to "waste them." And I directly—other than that—it was only that one incident. I never stood up there for any period of time. My main mission was to get my

men on the other side of that ditch and get in that defensive position and that's what I did, sir.

Q: Now why did you give Meadlo a message or the order that if he couldn't get rid of them to "waste them"?

A: Because that was my order. That was the order of the day.

Q: Who gave you that order?

A: My commanding officer, sir, Captain Medina, sir.

Q: And stated in that posture, in substantially those words, how many times did you receive such an order from Captain Medina?

A: The night before in the company briefing, the platoon leader's briefing, the following morning before we lifted off, and twice there in the village, sir . . .

Maj. Gen. Antonio M. Taguba penned a 53-page report that had not been intended for public release. In the report, the general noted that the intelligence people had insinuated that the Abu Ghraib prison guards should abuse the prisoners to soften them for subsequent interrogations. When one of the defendants was asked what Military Intelligence had said, he reported: "Loosen this guy up for us." "Make sure he has a bad night." "Make sure he gets the treatment." In return, defendants got compliments like: "Good job, they're breaking down real fast. They answer every question. They're giving out good information."

Only the guards at Abu Ghraib were prosecuted. They were all enlisted army personnel, primarily junior-enlisted.

The *Washington Post* reported that the techniques employed at Abu Ghraib resulting in prison time for eight of the nine enlisted defendants—techniques involving sexual humiliation, nudity, leashes, and snarling dogs—had in fact been employed three months prior at Guantánamo as part of an interrogation technique package approved by Defense Secretary Donald H. Rumsfeld for use in interrogating Mohamed Qahtani—the alleged "20th hijacker" in the 9/11 attack. The official report that the *Post* based its story on would seem to indicate that the abuses seen in photographs at Abu Ghraib were not the invention of a small group of thrill-seeking military police officers, but came from higher up.

Ramadi.

Graffito:
Bureaucracies can't kiss you cuz they ain't got lips

Although Rumsfeld approved a list of 16 harsh techniques for use at Guantánamo, most of the techniques have been called "general" and allowed for interpretation by interrogators.

Have you read *Lord of the Flies*?

My father took advantage of two horseflies copulating on the truck's dashboard to bring up the subject of sex.

Do you remember the film with Robin Williams in which as he's contemplating buying a house a small plane crashes into it? The agent signals the obvious: a plane sticking into the house. "And what are the chances of that happening again?" is the crux of the reaction. The agent has a point.

How to Write about Dead Fathers:
The things a man now keeps in the cab of a pickup truck: friction tape, jumper cables, county map, dinosaur bones, pliers, coffee mug with Town Pump logo, so many legal papers, letters to be mailed, maybe a tumbleweed or two, and, as we sharply turned the corner by the fairgrounds, a box, a small sealed cardboard box that slid along the dashboard all the way to the edge, struck the windshield, and fell to my feet. That's my dad, he said. —Jim Johnson, "The Things a Man Keeps"

I know more about the inner life of Hemingway's Jake Barnes or Melville's Ahab than I do about my brother Jim who I see drinking one last drink before he shoots himself as he reclines in the La-Z-Boy.

Sarin.

A Surefire Guide to Writing Successful Obituaries:

A deceased will generally *pass* or *exit* or *depart* this life. Useable synonyms for *life* are *afloat, under the sun, on the face of the earth, vale, sojourn, journey.*

Rather than *exit* life, one may *enter* heaven. Or: *God's heart/hands/ bosom. Afterworld, other world, next world, world to come. Gates,* of the *pearly* kind, *hereafter,* or the *Jesus Choir—Home of the Heavenly Host—Hallelujah!* Notions of *bliss, rapture,* and *contentment* are permissible, entirely. *Paradise* is a positive slant. Notions to avoid: *the unknown, the "great" unknown, the beyond, the grave, the abode of the dead.*

Deaths may be *unexpected* or *peaceful* or following *lengthy illnesses* and *battles* of the courageous sort. Deaths may be *natural* or *tragic and senseless.*

What death isn't *untimely*? (In death's world of cliché, *untimely* may have lost force from overuse. Skip *untimely.*)

If someone participated in the Normandy Invasion, or knows someone who did—mention it.

The deceased have loving personalities and traits, and will be *deeply* missed and *forever* loved.

Children may wing their ways *to the arms of a loving God,* and are generally thought of as *too perfect* to have remained on earth. (Children under the age of 12 may be referred to as *lambs.*)

When cojoined, *ultimate* and *sacrifice* are reserved for soldiers, cops, firefighters.

A young dead person should get credit for *fitting more life into his/ her limited years than others have managed to fit into their longer lives.* (What harm in this inaccurate statement? It should make everyone

feel better, and stir Uncle Earl off his deadbeat ass. Maybe.)

Men are golfers, woodworkers, sailors, and fishermen. They are sports fans, ham radio operators, Elks, Moose, Veterans of Foreign Wars, Masons, and servants of God. Women are chefs (normally pastry), bridge players, gardeners, listeners, bursars, and readers. As a rule of thumb, ALL deceased are *avid* and *experienced*.

USEFUL PHRASES—
until we meet again . . .
services are planned . . .
a better place . . .
had been an area resident . . .
still loved . . .
was preceded in death . . .
quietly / peacefully / naturally . . .
was a reasonably good cook . . .
of natural causes . . .
in lieu of flowers . . .
will be missed . . .
is survived by . . .

WORDS USED IN CONJUNCTION WITH DEAD WOMEN—
needle, bead, cat, crafts, jigsaw, devout/devoted, volunteer, quilt, sunflower, crossword, genealogy, Chihuahua, eggplant.

WORDS USED IN CONJUNCTION WITH DEAD MEN—
sheet metal, backpack, dog, tireless/hearty, saddle, fence, Purple Heart, purple pill, travel, extended cab, ammunition, Mastiff, derrick.

SAMPLE OBITS—
—for him
Eloy "Ed" Romero Jr., 86, was called to Heaven on May 29, 20xx after a courage-filled battle (with cancer) here on earth. "Ed" was born in Wagon Mound, New Mexico. "Ed" loved America and was proud to be an American. He proudly served his country in the United States Army during WWII in Africa and Europe. He married the love of

his life, Barbara Ruth, in Rancho de Taos in 1954 and together they had one child, Eloy Jr. "Ed" served 31 years in the Arroyo Seco Volunteer Fire Department, where as a community service he taught a semiannual CPR class. A dedicated member of the Church of Jesus Christ of Latter-Day Saints, "Ed" was a loving husband and family man and was preceded in death by his loving wife and his beloved and loving parents. "Ed" loved bait fishing, singing, and mountain air. On a heart transplant list for 15 years, "Ed" was, to the end of his life, an avid advocate for organ donation. "Ed" was an accomplished welder. His dream of becoming a chiropractor was realized by his granddaughter April (Ramos). "Ed" once bowled 282. A memorial service is pending.

—for her
Barbara "Babs" Mortenson, 63, of Cedar Falls, formally of Cedar Rapids, passed away quietly of natural causes complicated by organ failure on April 2, 20xx. Symbolizing what it means to be a true and caring friend, she has touched the lives of everyone with her loving personality and will be deeply missed and forever loved. Known to the best of her friends as "Babs," Barbara overcame polio and the early death of her husband, who preceded her in death. Even as the ravages of polio and stroke suppressed her mobility, Barbara continued to swim and maintained her membership at the Southside YMCA. As a teenager, she and her sister Lee (deceased) were popular singers of gospel music. In their youth, she and Lee (deceased) founded a soup kitchen that continues to this day, though it has been taken over by the Presbyterians. Barbara's husband Frank was an air force officer and they were stationed in Georgia, New Jersey, South Carolina, and England, where he died. Before he died, Frank and Barbara enjoyed cruising. Barbara was an excellent pastry chef. She loved needlework, sketching, and reading as well as her cats, especially the beloved "Kittyboots," who survives her. Frank and Barbara's union was blessed with four children. Like their mother, three of the four girls are master quilters. Barbara was a genealogical research enthusiast who traced her family history back to 1620 in Scotland. This sparked an interest for her to study Celtic and Egyptian culture. A highlight of Barbara's life was when, as a high school senior, she

met Rachel Carson, author of *Silent Spring*, the book denouncing the pesticide DDT. In lieu of flowers, donations may be made to the Humane Society or to the YMCA. Her sister parishioners at Holy Ghost Parish are preparing a needle tapestry depicting St. Florian (Barbara's favorite saint) to honor her. St. Florian was an officer in the Roman army who made a bold confession of his Christian conversion. He was twice scourged, half-flayed alive, set on fire, and finally thrown into the river Enns with a stone around his neck. His feast day is May 4th. Funeral arrangements by Blunt Mortuary.

—for them

Velcro was the best kitty in the world. I will always love her. You can see my tribute site at <http://velcro.htm> Vel, I love you.

Shug was a loving hamster full of life. He never bite anyone. He lead a long and joyful life of 2 and one-half years. R.I.P.

Appendix:

1. SAMPLE USEFUL BAD POEMS—

Today is the day I wish you were here.
Yet today is the day I will not shed a tear.
Because today is the day I will not want to mourn.
For today is the day,
The day you were born.

No farewell words were spoken
No time to say goodbye
You were gone before we knew
It and only God knows why.

Our family chain is broken, and
Nothing seems the same,
But as God calls us one by one,
The chain will link again.

2. MISCELLANY—

A local survey reported 20xx obituary rates as follows:

1–50 words: $53.25.

51–100 words: $94.00.

101–200 words: $166.75.

201–300 words: $231.50.

301 or more words: 75¢ per word.

Photos: $12.50.

Logos and emblems: $10.00.

Pet Obituaries, starting at $25.00.

3. COMMONLY, OBITUARIES MUST BE PREPAID—

Four times as many soldiers died in World War II than in World War I, 405,000 to 117,000. Vietnam contributed 58,000 to Korea's 37,000. The First Gulf War was nearly a video game, or so it appeared on TV. A few less than 400 died. This second excursion into Iraq (and Afghanistan) is moving toward 6,000 deaths. There are numerous sites on the Internet where you can click on "Age," "Year of Death," "Home State," "Military Branch," etc. You can click on faces. You can know them all.

At the moment, the Afghanistan War costs (*all* costs) come to $3.6 billion per month. The costs get pegged at about $1 million per soldier per year.

The Vietnam War cost $686 billion.

The 38th parallel is insignificant in either Korean geography or culture. It was designated at the end of World War II to facilitate the surrender of Japanese troops simply because it appeared on most maps. Japanese troops north of the line surrendered to the Soviet Union; those south of it surrendered to the United States.

The Criminal Investigation Command (CID) deposition files from the My Lai investigation document 20 rapes during the assault—among the victims, the youngest was 11, the oldest 45.

From the Testimony of Herbert L. Carter:
The first killing was an old man in a field outside the village who said some kind of greeting in Vietnamese and waved his arms at us. Someone—either Medina or Calley—said to kill him and a big heavy-set white fellow killed the man. I do not know the name of the man who shot this Vietnamese. This was the first murder.

Only the dead have seen the end of war. —Plato

From the Testimony of Michael Terry:
 Q: Did you fire on wounded civilians?
 A: OK, I will explain. There were some people—you remember the area I told you about where they were rounded up and shot down?
 Q: Yes.
 A: When we came up to that area, our platoon came up to that area, we were right in that area and there were some people there that we couldn't tell if they were dead or not. Well, a couple of them must not have been dead because they kept whipping around and their heads had been blown off or their brains were sticking out and it was a sickening sight, their limbs were just wiggling, and I remember we shot a couple of those.
 Q: Why?
 A: Our intent in doing this was—I mean there was no way that they could live and so we just tried to make it faster for them.
 Q: How do you know that?
 A: When half of their head is missing or their brains sticking out, and for one thing we didn't judge them in any way, but no helicopters were called in there to evacuate the wounded or anything and they just left them laying there and they would just move ahead.
 Q: What was your duty assignment?
 A: My duty assignment was team leader.
 Q: Who was with you when this incident took place?
 A: This specific one I just mentioned?
 Q: Yes.
 A: Bill Doherty . . .
 Q: Was he a subordinate of yours?
 A: Yes, there were about three guys under me.
 Q: Did you order him to do this?

*A: I don't think you could say I ordered him to do it in any way. I mean
we just kind of did it by ourselves, you know, on our own.*

Q: Did you kill these civilians?

A: Did we kill them? I don't know if you could construe it to say that.

During World War II, Japanese leadership had ordered children evacu-
ated from the cities. At the same time, all men and women 15 and older
were ordered to enroll in the militia. With a "defense" force of 50 mil-
lion, the Japanese ruling clique hoped to make the Americans think
twice about invasion. A by-product was to make American air raids on
Japanese cities a "legitimate" act of war, as the cities were now "military
installations." U.S. incendiaries burned the wooden and paper Japanese
cities like willing tinder, inducing firestorms that melted people.

Even with records being as they are, most experts agree that some
number over 600,000 soldiers died in the American Civil War. Some
experts, citing poor Confederate records, argue for a number closer
to 700,000—in other words, more than all our other wars combined.

Chosin.

After 85 days, 16 hours, 25 seconds, and an estimated 184,000,000 gal-
lons of oil later, BP stops the hemorrhaging with a 75-ton cap. A vice
president of BP was quoted on the day of the capping as saying he was
excited, *very excited there was no oil in the Gulf of Mexico.*

Gulf crabbers were less buoyant: . . . *putting a Band-Aid on a dead
man . . .*

Ileus:

*Impairment of the caudad flow of the intestinal contents. Symptoms are
a function of the level of obstruction and the type of ileus. Paralytic ileus
is first evident through abdominal distention and vomiting.*

My father spent the last half of his career in the mines as a safety en-
gineer. Just before he retired, he removed two fingers dislodging wet
grass from under a running mower.

Entr'acte

I spent more time in the hospital to reconnect my colon than I did for the visit when it originally burst. At rest six months, my bowels had forgotten their work. And then there was the morphine that, in doing its work, paralyzed the gut.

When I woke after the first surgery, one of the cheers had been the available drugs. I was IVed into a drug machine I controlled. Computerized, the machines wouldn't permit overdose. But: You were in charge—didn't have to wait or ask for a nurse. I've been since informed that research supports that patients in charge of their own narcotics use less. But what I knew then—*and know now*—requires no study: whatever pain has to teach is unworthy. Pain has nothing to do with faith or hope or character.

Each day after the second surgery, I felt worse. I was informed that my body's wastes were rising and that my reconnected bowels misunderstood. I began to projectile vomit. The force of it all seemed dangerous, and the pain from the heaves made me sweat. The nausea caused by the constantly building bile felt impossible to face. I was weeping when the head nurse came into my room with equipment. She had a six-foot tube coiled in ice in a rectangular tray. The tube was transparent. Nurse sat me upright in a straight-backed chair in the center of the room and began feeding the tube up my right nostril. She'd asked if I had a preference, left? right?

The tube had been packed in the ice to stiffen—but not too stiff—because, as Nurse pointed out, it had to make the turn to descend by way of the throat to the stomach. The tube being force-wormed down my throat worsened all. Nurse kept saying, "Help me, Mr. Anderson." She had me nipping at water from a mini-cup. In theory, this sacramental nipping was to help me to not resist the tube. In time, the tube was installed by way of my left nostril (Nurse abandoning the attempt through the right), down my throat, to and through the cardia, into the well of my stomach. I wept throughout the procedure.

Returned to my bed, I was connected to some sort of jar and suction. I watched the silage from my stomach travel through the tube to its new container. As before, I was IVed into my own narcotics. But despite this availability, I was unable to sleep, what with the tube poled in my throat, and the pain of the surgeon's most recent invasion. Flesh had

torn at the staples during the powerful vomiting. Blood beaded along the length of the incision.

Coates came by on his morning round: "Sorry—this usually occurs."

"What?" It wasn't easy to talk.

"The stomach pump—whatnot."

"If it usually happens, why didn't you install the tube before I came out of surgery, while I was asleep? Christ, Coates—you know? Had a tube in me the first time. Am I right?"

"That was an emergency. There was food in your gut—we didn't want you vomiting under gas. As for now—well—all patients don't need to be pumped. It doesn't *always* happen."

"No, just *usually*," I said.

"You need to wean off the painkiller. Narcotics paralyze and we need the bowels to wake up. The pump here'll keep the sewage down, but we need the bowels to wake up."

"And the pain?"

"Have to choose," Coates said. "Up to you. The sooner the bowels rouse, the sooner we jerk the pump. The sooner we can jerk it." He lifted the jar as if to study the sludge. "I know it's no fun."

"I may have opted for the shit bag had I known what fun." I ask for a shot for nausea. I wanted something out of the visit.

It took three days for my bowels to rouse.

Over a period of weeks, the hole in my belly closed.—from "Luck," *Fire Road*

Two weeks following prostate surgery, my father climbed a tree to trim some top branches. He fell from the tree, broke his leg.

The acid in your stomach could dissolve a spoon, but don't eat glass. A friend of mine's baby sister ate a Christmas ornament and died.

On the day he died, Donald Arthur Anderson stirred up four heart attacks in 14 hours. He had a job to do, and he did it.

Maalox.

Entr'acte

When I dream, I am a boy with my father in my uncle's car, an old Chrysler with FluidDrive. It is unclear where we are headed in my uncle's blue car, but in the dream we are crossing Kansas. My father shakes me awake to see, in the distance, an overpass. My father, wobbled by the construction, wants me to see it. The overpass grows until we pass beneath it. My father threatens to stop my uncle's car. What he does is accelerate. There is a scent of something. I know because it's hot and the windows are rolled down. "Get your head in here," my father shouts, still mashing the gas. Then he softens, sends me to the back seat to look through that window.

The overpass has been perfectly constructed except that there are no roads to it—the bridge connects air. Each time I turn, my father's still glaring at this shoreless bridge in his mirror. He doesn't complain I'm blocking his view.

In time, the bridge drops below the horizon. My father backs off on the gas. He calls me to the front seat to explain the bridge disappears because the earth is not flat, but round. "Even Kansas," he says. He seems surprised himself.

My guess is the bridge is real—that I saw it with my father. That if I were to drive along long enough in Kansas, I'd sight it. Somewhere near Junction City, say, or Salina, or Wilson Lake, or Hays. The bridge would arrive. Or I would.

The perfect pointless construction astraddle a road, triumphantly idle: a sundial centered for a nation, an altar, a permanent needle of a compass facing north, an Andy Warhol joke, a perch for bird or locust, an unfinished road from home.—from "Barrie Hooper's Dead," *Fire Road*

PART

II

Two pugs on the undercard step through
The ropes in satin robes,
Pink Adidas with tassels,
Winking at the women in the crowd.
At instructions they stare down hard
And refuse to touch their gloves,
Trying to make everyone believe
That this will be a serious dust-up.

But when the bell rings they start
Slapping like a couple of Barbie dolls.
One throws a half-hearted hook,
The other flicks out a jab,
They bounce around for a while
Then grab each other for a tango.
The crowd gets tired of booing
And half of them go out for a beer,
But I've got no place to hide.

A week after a cancer scare,
A year from a detached retina,
Asthmatic, overweight, trickling,
Drooling, bent like a blighted elm
In my pajamas and slippers,
I have turned up my hearing aids to sit in
Numbness without expectation before
These televised Tuesday Night Fights.

With a minute left in the fourth,
Scuffling, they butt their heads
By accident. In the midst of all the catcalls
And hubbub suddenly they realize
How much they hate each other.

They start hammering and growling,
Really dealing, whistling combinations,
Hitting on the breaks and thumbing.
At last one guy crosses a stiff jab
With a roundhouse right and the other
Loses his starch. The guy wades into
The wounded one, pounding him
Back and forth until he goes down,
Bouncing his head hard on the canvas.

The count begins but he is saved
By the bell and his trainers haul
Him to his stool as the lens zooms in.

I come to the edge of my La-Z-Boy,
Blinking and groaning from my incision,
Eager for wise, insightful instruction.

He gets a bucket of water in his face,
A sniff on the salts while the cutman
Tries to close his wounds with glue.
His nose is broken, eyes are crossed,
His lips bleed like two rare steaks.
His cornermen take turns slapping his cheeks.
"Suck it up!" they shout.
"Suck it up!"

—PAUL ZIMMER, *Suck It Up*

Our most ancient metaphor says that life is a journey.
Memoir is travel writing, then, notes taken along the way,
telling how things looked and what thoughts occurred.
—PATRICIA HAMPL, Memory and Imagination

A friend of ours died yesterday after a yearlong bout with Stage 4 terminal brain cancer. Three weeks before she passed, she awoke with terrible pain and had to submit to a root canal.

I will tell you something about stories. . . . They aren't just for entertainment. Don't be fooled. They are all we have . . . to fight off illness and death. You don't have anything if you don't have the stories.—Leslie Marmon Silko

Entr'acte

In the fall of 1987, a deer struck my car. Never saw the deer. It may as well have been a meteorite or a bullet. What I heard was the noise. Though the deer had been inside the car, I never saw it. My door was jammed, but I don't remember crawling over the gear shift to exit on the passenger side. I do remember staring at my Bronco II, wondering why all the windows were gone and why the interior was gore. To stare at this, I'd had to thumb my eyeglasses clean. It looked as if there had been people in the car and that a bomb had gone off. But I'd been the sole passenger and in the one place inside the vehicle that'd been safe. Any passenger in any other seat would have been killed. As it was explained to me by someone who'd seen, the deer had bounded down from the mesa, leaped over two cars driving side-by-side in the other direction, then dropped from the sky onto the post separating the front windshield and my driver's door window. Halved, but held together by its spine, the deer then wheeled like a nunchuk into the left-side vista window, whirled

about within the car, breaking every window, slashing the headliner, then exiting through the smashed out right-side vista window. The deer had entered my car and then left it. By the time I got the car slowed and off the highway, I'd traveled blind 100 yards from the carcass. My windshield was the only glass intact, though it had spidered and folded in like a browned quilt. The halved, whirling deer had emptied its cavity inside the Bronco. I, the upholstery, and dash were covered.

The tow truck agreed to drive me home, as it was on his way. He did give my shirt and pants a good look and I did my best not to lean back in his truck seat. I held my briefcase, and two other shirts and a suit I'd meant to drive to the cleaners. Everything slimed. A neighbor who saw the Bronco being towed assumed I was dead. My next-door neighbor told me I stood on my curb after Mr. Tow Truck left. I headed up my driveway toward the garage, lifted the lid from the garbage and dumped the briefcase, suit, shirts. I next stripped, dumped all that in the can. Naked in my own backyard, I ran the garden hose on my head, then on my hands and two shoes. I gargled hose water. When I woke in the morning, there were streaks on my sheets. Glass in my hair had cut me. Careful as I was, when I washed my hair in the shower, I nicked my fingers.—from "Luck," *Fire Road*

As an adult, I did and didn't want to confirm my grandfather's story about his sparring with Jack Dempsey. As it turns out, my grandfather was the right age to do it and was then living in Colorado, a train ride from Manassa.

The day of the accident, I'd left work early.

When my father was a kid, he watched his father defeat a local tough. In a ring in the Butte Civic Center, my grandfather stepped through the ropes in his work shoes and stripped off his shirt. He wore long pants and a belt. Gloved-up, he took more than he gave, then one-eyed—one eye punched shut—jockeyed a right that knocked a fighter called Dixie LaHood senseless. In the center of the Depression, my grandfather stepped out of the ring, barechested, took his shirt and earnings, then walked home with my father, his son. How many chances like that does a father have?

102

Can the head, my grandfather advised, *Bomb the gut. You can change your luck*, he said, *if you hard-bang the body. Bomb the gut.* He gave me this advice in the county home. Two weeks later, he died.

Early on, I wrote a story about my father and grandfather. An editor who rejected it, wrote: "This is a story that purports to be about love, but it's really about people who hit each other."

When I was 12, my father was on his knees on canvas sacking he'd brought home from the mines and we were boxing. Somehow I sneaked one through and bloodied his nose. The bloom on his face shocked me.

I lived on nothing but dreams and train smoke . . .
—Tom Waits, from "Pony"

My Father on Women:
You can be right, or you can be happy.

From the Testimony of Max D. Hutson:
The night prior to the mission . . . CPT Medina called the company to-gether and explained the mission to us. He stated that My Lai #4 was a suspected strong hold and that he had orders to kill everybody that was in the village. We did not expect to find anyone in the village, and when we did, we did as ordered.

At one time Jack Dempsey shared an apartment with Charlie Chaplin and Douglas Fairbanks Sr.

In Midwestern farmlands rustling wheatcrowns,
spreading out with alfalfa and sorghum, sprouting corn,
I thought I was lost, in the crickets and songbirds,
But tire whine and bumper glare kept me on course
and when I picked up the soldier mugged in the bus station,
teeth kicked in, wallet taken, hitching back to base in Waco
to his tank-repair unit readying for another Iraq war
I knew I was on the right road, running like a lifeline
across the palm of America.
—John Balaban, from "Highway 61 Revisited"

103

If you were a poor Indian with no weapons, and a bunch of conquistadors came up to you and asked where the gold was, I don't think it would be a good idea to say, "I swallowed it. So sue me."—Jack Handey

Is Jack Handey an individual or a committee? Do you know?

Vanity of vanities, saith the preacher; all is vanity . . .

If I lived back in the wild west days, instead of carrying a six-gun in my holster, I'd carry a soldering iron. That way, if some smart-aleck cowboy said something like "Hey, look. He's carrying a soldering iron!" and started laughing, and everybody else started laughing, I could just say, "That's right, it's a soldering iron. The soldering iron of justice." Then everybody would get real quiet and ashamed, because they had made fun of the soldering iron of justice, and I could probably hit them up for a free drink.—Jack Handey

If you can believe Wikipedia, Jack Handey *is* an individual born in 1949, but how can we be sure the committee didn't write the entry?

One more: *Sometimes when I feel like killing someone, I do a little trick to calm myself down. I'll go over to the person's house and ring the doorbell. When the person comes to the door, I'm gone, but you know what I've left on the porch? A jack-o-lantern with a knife stuck in the side of its head with a note that says "You." After that I usually feel a lot better, and no harm done.*

Did Gordon Lish rewrite Ray Carver's stories?

From the Testimony of Paul Meadlo:
From the first day we go in the service, the very first day, we are learned to take orders and not to refuse any kind of order from a noncommissioned officer or an officer would give, and that means even that if you stand on your head. An officer tells you to go and stand on your head, it's not your right to refuse that order, and you go out there and do it because you're ordered to. It's more or less in combat that it's more so there, because all through the service you hear rumors that in World War II there was

people that picked up and ran, and there was officers that would shoot
their men in the head to stop their people from running too. All right. You
don't know what's going to come off. If you refuse the order, the son-of-
a-bitch might shoot you or the next day you spend the rest of your life in
the stockade for refusing an order, but you're trained to take orders from
the first day you go to that damned service, and you come back and, all
right, you want to try some people that had to take orders.

A famous and pretty female writer is said to have said to Lish at a party,
"If you want to say you've bedded me, go ahead, Gordon, but don't ever
tell anyone that I admire your writing."

As for Calley, he was sentenced to life for the murder of Vietnamese
civilians (reported by some as an "unspecified number"). The lieuten-
ant's life sentence was immediately reviewed and reduced to 20 years.
The secretary of the army then reduced it to 10. The three years Calley
did serve were under house arrest. He is reported to be working in his
father-in-law's jewelry store in Georgia.

In his memoirs, Richard Nixon reports that the White House received
thousands of telegrams running 100 to 1 in favor of clemency for Calley.

From the Testimony of Herbert L. Carter:
. . . Calley had two Vietnamese with him at this time and he killed them,
too, by shooting them with his M16 rifle on automatic fire. I didn't want
to get involved and I walked away. There was no reason for this killing.
These were mainly women and children and a few old men. They weren't
trying to escape or attack or anything. It was murder.
 A woman came out of a hut with a baby in her arms and she was
crying. She was crying because her little boy had been in front of her hut
and someone had killed the child by shooting it. She came out of her hut
with her baby and Widmer shot her with an M16 and she fell. When she
fell, she dropped the baby and then Widmer opened up on the baby with
his M16 and killed the baby, too.
 I also saw another woman come out of a hut and Calley grabbed her
by the hair and shot her with a caliber .45 pistol. He held her by the hair
for a minute and then let go and she fell to the ground.

In his memoirs, Nixon continues: *I think most Americans understood that the My Lai massacre was not representative of our people, of the war we were fighting, or of our men who were fighting it; but from the time it first became public the whole tragic episode was used by the media and the antiwar forces to chip away at our efforts to build public support for our Vietnam objectives and policies.*

In 2004, journalists Michael Sallah and Mitch Weiss won the Pulitzer Prize for Investigative Reporting for their story about Tiger Force, a group of elite soldiers who went on a seven-month rampage. This "sanctioned" murder spree was buried for 40 years.

The upshot of the revelation about the disgraceful fall of Tiger Force is that the unit was formed and supported with leadership's full knowledge, including Westmoreland. The idea was small mobile units with on-site command and self-sufficiency. The founder of the Tigers was Colonel David Hackworth, who was the model for *Apocalypse Now*'s Colonel Kilgore.

"I want 40 swinging dicks," Hackworth told a reporter. Without bureaucracy or constant requests for permission, Hackworth intended to "outguerrilla the guerrillas." The unit was to actively find the enemy, engage the enemy, and destroy the enemy. Period. *I want 40 swinging dicks . . .*

I love the smell of napalm in the morning.
—Colonel Kilgore, *Apocalypse Now*

As some planners for Military Assitance Command, Vietnam (MACV) worried, the small-unit Tigers began to take the war into their own hands, but in the Vietnam numbers game, the Tigers showed progress. Higher-ups recorded the numbers.

Robert Duval.

Sgt. William Doyle was considered one of the more ruthless Tiger Force team leaders. Unashamed of his participation, he chafed that others

would confess to crimes. "If I walked into a village and everyone wasn't lying prostrate on the ground, I shot those standing up. If they didn't understand fear, I taught it to them. We were living day to day. We didn't expect to live. We were surprised to be alive next week. So you did any goddamn thing you felt like doing—especially to stay alive. I'm not saying you give up and die. You struggle to live. But the way to live is to kill, because you don't have to worry about anybody who is dead."

Sergeant Doyle bragged about killing unarmed men, women, and children—noncombatants.

"I only wish I killed more."

Watch how you vote . . .

Tiger Force was the last major war-crime investigation from Vietnam. A summary of CID's ongoing investigation was forwarded to the offices of Howard "Bo" Calloway, secretary of the army, and James Schlesinger, secretary of defense. When reporters Sallah and Weiss called these two individuals, and others who had served during that period, they were stonewalled.

LeMay couldn't smile . . .

Kool-Aid.

Tang.

Thomas McGuane on Texas:
Texas is . . . a place where Birkenstocks, oat bran, foreign films and Saabs spontaneously catch fire and then smolder grimly in an alien climate.

Collage, the art of reassembling fragments of the preexisting images in such a way as to form a new image, was the most important innovation in the art of the twentieth century . . .—David Shields, reflecting on Charles Simic reflecting on Joseph Cornell

At the Alamo there were overweight women in puffy clothes, speaking in concentrated drawls. Mexicans were at work in the gardens, thinning ice plant. I was handed a brochure listing the heroic dead: Jim Bowie, Davy Crockett, etc. The dead soldiers were all listed by name, rank, year of birth, city and state. For example: *Peter James Bailey III; Private; 1812; Springfield, Kentucky.* The final entry read: *John, Negro.*

Of the 189 Alamo defenders officially listed as killed, only one was buried. José Gregorio Esparza, a Hispanic, was interred. The rest were burned. The interment came by way of special permission of Santa Anna himself.

Prep H.

Pez.

As I have said, I saw no deer fall from the sky. In fact, I thought I'd been shot, what with the noise and gore. What I saw didn't occur. I saw—*and it is crystal clear*—an old-model Oldsmobile pull up (rust in the wheel wells), barreling south beside me. The hood was pitted. The passenger, who'd been bent toward the floor mat, straightened, raising a shotgun, and then there was glass shattering, blood and flesh chunks, and the echoing report of the fired weapon. *This* is what I saw and heard, not a deer falling from the sky to enter, then exit, my car.

A smell like wet hay and copper.

. . . imagination and memory are so interconnected (PET scans, for example, show that the same areas of the brain are affected, whether we imagine or experience something), it might at first glance seem handy to connect the two names with a hyphen, in the manner of certain present-day marriage partners. But in this case memory is no doubt the dominant partner, and must provide the family name. Still, there is a dalliance between the pair, one necessary for literature.—James McConkey

It's a poor sort of memory that only works backwards . . .

The week earlier at the location where I struck the deer, there had been a shooting. A driver had cut off another in traffic and a chase had ensued. The pursuing driver forced the other driver off the shoulder, then fired at the car seven times. One of the slugs killed the driver. The shooter was an unemployed electronics worker. He was black, the dead man white—all milked on local TV.

It's not the word made flesh that we want in writing . . . but the flesh made word.—William Gass

. . . every loving act of definition reverses the retreat of attention to the word and returns it to the world. The landscape which emerges from the language which has made it is quite as lovely, vast and curious, as rich and prepossessing, as that of the deity who broke the silence of the void with speech so perfect the word "tree" grew leaves and the syllables of "sealion" swallowed fish.—Ibid.

The imagination will make sense of what it thinks it knows . . .

The two-man luge?

The world shrieks and sinks talons into our hearts. This we call memory.
—Tim O'Brien, qtd. in Herzog

Colorado. I live in a state where if someone lights up in a Noel Coward play, someone in the audience is liable to call the police and have the actor dragged from the stage and arrested.

In the mountain town in which I breathe, folks walk llamas like Manhattanites walk poodles.

I saw the best minds of my generation destroyed by madness . . .

Buddy Holly, Richie Valens, the Big Bopper.

(Oh, Baby, you KNOW what I like!)

Clint Eastwood as Rowdy Yates.

After 40 years, I have reread, this summer, all of Faulkner. There is, of course, much to admire, but where do we get the idea that long-dead authors are best? To tell you the truth, I'd rather read Cormac McCarthy than William Faulkner. And there are any number of short-story writers I'd rather read than Papa H. Alice Munro, for instance, or William Trevor, or Tobias Wolff, or Raymond Carver. Richard Ford can write, and Frederick Busch, and Ernest Gaines. Georges of the Saunders or Singleton sort? Darrell Spencer? Lee K. Abbott—have you read Abbott? V. S. Pritchett?

That's what fiction is for. It's for getting at the truth when the truth isn't sufficient for the truth.—Tim O'Brien, qtd. in Herzog

Peggy Sue.

Our cars are safer, medicines improved, roofs long-lasting. We have hot water heaters and birth control. Prilosec and Viagra. We run faster, jump higher. Probe space. Have you seen *Avatar*—at IMAX? We're taller. Why wouldn't we be better writers?

To me, boxing is like a ballet, except there's no music, no choreography, and the dancers hit each other.—Jack Handey

Does anyone work with fewer words better than Jack Handey?

Colorado is the thinnest state of the 50 principalities, Mississippi the stoutest.

In my state, the quick route to sophistication is a beard, a backpack, and a mountain bike.

In Colorado, you can buy mountain bikes with a single gear.

Bobby Darin.

Boulder Daughter's Definition of a Granola:
Someone who wears Birkenstocks in the winter, eschews nail polish, and glares at Styrofoam . . .

What the Doctor Said before the Cortisone Shot into the Sole of My Foot:
You might notice this . . .

Entr'acte

I was on my back, nude, but for my socks, from the waist down. My scrotum had been shaved and painted orange, like a baboon's ass. My feet were in stirrups. I was an air force major at the time, stationed in DC. The surgeon's assistant, a pretty little sergeant named Wendy, comported herself as if this was a natural occurrence for three strangers. I'd received the numbing shot and the full-bird colonel urologist was being especially polite as he was about to cut and tie fisherman's knots in my vas deferens. Throughout, the colonel kept addressing me as "Major," even though I'd shown up in civilian clothes. I was wishing I'd worn black instead of bright argyle socks, anything to render the procedure less festive. Wendy had arranged a green cloth over my middle, with an opening, as if the orange disinfectant hadn't narrowed the options.

"Major," the colonel said, "you're about now to feel somewhat of a tug." He was grunting a bit, but with an English accent.

"Charles," I said, "*STOP*." The colonel straightened and we made eye contact, eyeball to pestered eyeball.

"There are times, Charles, when all men are brothers. Stop calling me 'Major.'"

When he finished, Charles wrote a prescription for Vicodin, but said, in his view, the best bet was a bag of frozen peas.

"I think you'll find," he said, "the peas are best." He was suggesting, I gathered, that if I stayed off the narcotic painkiller, I could drink, which seemed reasonable to me: cold peas and gin.

Repeated injections of cortisone weakens tissue over time, making one even more susceptible to failure.

I had torn off my side-view mirror on a concrete pillar in the under-ground garage at my workplace. On a blizzard day—18 inches of snow and high winds—schools and government offices had closed, and I was home from work. I called WRECKMASTERS: *Wreckmasters—Jimbo here.* "So you're there," I said. "I wondered." *Our kind of weather*, Jimbo said.

This history of mine has from the beginning sought out the supplementary to the main argument.—Herodotus

From the Department of Advice:
Marry someone with the same age equipment . . .

Here's One You've Heard:
Don't eat at a place called "Mom's," don't play cards with a man named "Slim," and don't go to bed with a person who has more problems than you do . . .

Batista.

What is history if not humans running toward war or from it?

Before he became a joke, Burt Reynolds in *Deliverance*.

"I know death, now. . . . I know all the smells, I know how to divert them from agony. When to give the quick jolt of morphine in a major vein. The saline solution. To make them empty their bowels before they die. Every damn general should have had my job. Every damn general. It should have been a prerequisite for any river crossing. Who the hell were we to be given this responsibility, expected to be wise as old priests, to know how to lead people towards something no one wanted and somehow make them feel comfortable. I could never believe in all those services they gave for the dead. Their vulgar rhetoric. How dare they! How dare they talk like that about a human being dying."—Hana, the 20-year-old nurse in Michael Ondaatje's *The English Patient*

Princess Phones.

Chubby Checkers.

When I was 6, my grandfather walked me up Butte's Main Street to the *Rialto*. We watched Tony Curtis in the *Son of Ali Baba*. I remember Tony swimming underwater, escaping. I see the bubbles from his mouth and then his breathing through a reed (how cool!). On our way back down the hill, Grandpa in his long-sleeved, red union underwear, bib overalls, and sweat-creased fedora, peeled off at the M&M, a 24-hour bar near the mines. I walked on to Grandma's alone. I'd watched Grandpa turn in onto the sawdusted floor, where he became suddenly content and lively. Men were shouting his name. He was breathing.

One-eyed, one-horned, flying purple people eater . . .

At Grandma's, I wolfed a bowl of Corn Chex.

The good people of this wirld [sic] are very far from being satisfied with each other & my arms are the best peacemakers.—Samuel Colt (1814–62)

Entr'acte
Samuel Colt's early interest in firearms and explosives resulted in the torching of Amherst Academy. At 16, Colt designed a Fourth of July fireworks display. His school was burned to the ground. Expecting expulsion, Colt fled Hartford and signed on as a merchant seaman. It was the operation of the ship's capstan that provided Colt with the idea for a revolving cylinder.

Having seen Calcutta, Colt toured New England as an 18-year-old traveling salesman. Calling himself "Dr." Colt, he sold nitrous oxide (laughing gas), and with his earnings began to build prototypes of his revolver, an invention that would alter history, though Colt's first try at manufacturing revolvers had ended in bankruptcy. A failure at 28, Colt turned his attention to waterproof ammunition and underwater mines for harbor defense. This project was in association with Samuel F. B. Morse, the inventor of the telegraph.

Then, Colt's first revolver factory still closed, Texas Ranger Captain Samuel Walker publicly credited the use of Colt firearms for the

Rangers' success in defeating the Indians. With the start of the Mexican War, Capt. Walker traveled east to collaborate with Colt on the design of an improved and more powerful revolver. Back in the firearms business, now "Colonel" Colt teamed up with Eli Whitney Jr., son of the famed inventor. Together with Elisha King Root (he who brought the mass production of axes to perfection), they engineered a high-speed automated production line that would prove inspiration to Henry Ford himself.

Though he was to die before the Colt Firearms Company hit its stride, Colt, nonetheless, at age 47, was one of the 10 wealthiest businessmen in the United States. He produced over 400,000 weapons during his life. In the 170 years following his invention, some 30 million revolvers, pistols, and rifles bearing the Colt name have been produced. His weapons (from the *Walker* to the *Dragoon*, to the *Wells Fargo*, to the *Navy*, and the *Single Action Army*—the *"Peacemaker,"* to the *Gatling*, the *BAR*, the *Officer's Model .45*, and the *M16*, to today's *M4* specifically designed for close-quarters combat) have been present in every American war since that skirmish in Mexico.—from "Plus ça change . . ."

Gunpowder is an ancient invention (ninth-century China).

Quick Take:
For me, growing up, Mormon doctrine, as I understood it, was that blacks were black as a consequence of God's curse on Cain. The notion being that, having murdered his brother Abel, Cain was then struck with a blackened skin so that any who found him would know *not* to kill him (God meaning for Cain to suffer a long and harried existence). One of Noah's sons, Ham, then married a daughter of Cain. From that marriage sprang, in Joseph Smith's words, "a race which preserved the curse in the land."

"And the sins of the fathers shall be
visited upon the heads of the children,
even unto the third and fourth
generation of them that hate me."

Well, then I hate thee, unrighteous picture;
Wicked image, I hate thee;
So, strike with Thy vengeance
The heads of those little men
Who come blindly.
It will be a brave thing.
—Stephen Crane

Quick Take:
In the Church's *Book of Mormon*, white skin is lauded. According to Smith and his book, "Lamanites" (or Native Americans) are said to be cursed with a darker skin because of sin and disobedience. Long before the arrival of Columbus, "righteous" whites warred with their darker-skinned brethren. Eventually the whites (called "Nephites") fell into their own sinful ways and were slaughtered by the Lamanites. Moroni (who these days adorns in golden form—trumpet to lips—most Mormon temples worldwide) was, by his own account, a couple hundred years after the coming and going of Christ, the last righteous white man standing in the Americas. (By the by, according to the *Book of Mormon*, Jesus, himself, dropped in for a visit to the Americas right after his death and resurrection in the Old Country. Hence, the *Book of Mormon* and its notion of an "American" religion.)

1492. The same year Columbus sailed his blue ocean, Spanish Jews were issued the ultimatum to convert or be expelled.

Wernher von Braun.

Quick Take:
The prophet Moroni guarded, then buried, the Golden Plates, an abridgment of the records about Christ and the people of the Americas—"a remnant of the house of Israel"—only to return in angel form in a visitation to Joseph Smith in upstate New York in 1823, at which time he informs the 14-year-old Smith of the existence of the Golden Plates. (Moroni was not the first to appear to the teenager. Smith claimed that God and Jesus did, too.) Four years after his first visit (the same year during which Beethoven dies), the Angel Moroni releases the Golden

115

Plates to Smith. As you may have guessed, the Golden Plates, translated by young Joseph into the *Book of Mormon*, were, translation complete, returned to Moroni and the heavens.

Gary Powers.

Overheard in a Used Record Store:
Ma, Paul McCartney was with a group before Wings!

My grandmother cooked on a wood stove, which also heated the back of the house. A small gas stove heated the front part. Its face featured an isinglass window through which you could see flame, as if peering into a kaleidoscope.

The "iceman" toted in block ice for my grandmother's refrigerator. He carried the ice with tongs on his shoulder, on leather shoulder padding. There was sawdust on the ice and on the iceman's shoulder. His tongs were blackened, as if left in a fire.

And This:
Spencer W. Kimball, the LDS prophet on watch when blacks were admitted to the priesthood was, as well, a booster of the "Indian Placement Program," wherein "Indians" from reservations were placed into white Mormon foster homes. He pronounced on the subject: "I saw a striking contrast in the progress of the Indian people today as against that of only 15 years ago. Truly the scales of darkness are falling from their eyes, and they are fast becoming a white and delightsome people."

My grandmother had a phonograph, playing 45s, 78s, 33 1/3s: Louis Armstrong and Diana Washington, Les Paul and Mary Ford, Patsy Cline, Eddy Arnold, Jim Reeves, Frankie Avalon, Johnny Tillotson, Petula Clark. She'd buy 45s by singers she saw on Ed Sullivan. She skipped the Beatles.

Bob Beamon's success at the Mexico City Summer Olympics and Jim Ryun's failure, both due to the thin-aired altitude.

Hi-Fi.

Tommie Smith and John Carlos were banned from the Olympics for life for their quiet, black-gloved fist pump. The third-place finisher, an Australian who wore an American "civil rights" badge to support his running mates, was left off the Australian 1972 Olympic team.

1968. The first Olympic disqualification because of doping: Swedish pentathlete Hans-Gunnar Liljenwall was disqualified for drinking beer prior to his competition.

Annette Funicello.

Should we distinguish between hope and belief?

Should people who die aboard a spaceship be treated as if more essential than people who die aboard a bus?

Ollie North.

Daniel Ellsberg.

Joseph Smith claimed to have employed two translucent stones or crystals to translate the *Book of Mormon* from its ancient tongue. These stones, affixed to a breastplate so Smith could gaze through them at the Golden Plates, were named *Urim* and *Thummin*, after their predecessors in the Old Testament. But as a kid, *Urim* and *Thummin* sounded to me like something out of Tolkien. My father read to us from *The Hobbit*, a book he'd encountered as a reading teenager. He liked stories about dwarves and goblins and wizards. And so did we. At the time, Golden Plates and seer-stones made perfect sense to me. As did otherworldly personages appearing in blinding light.

WikiLeak.

Kandahar.

There is a website comparing champion killers: Hitler, Mao, Stalin—but how do you pick the winner? Is Hitler responsible for 6 million dead Jews or for the nearly 50 million dead Europeans? Do you get extra credit (or no credit) for killing your own people, as did Mao and Stalin? For sheer numbers, Stalin would probably be crowned champ, far outscoring underachievers such as Saddam Hussein who dispatched a mere million. For productive, cost-effective slaughter, though, you have to hand it to the Rwandans.

Decimation means the killing of every tenth person in a population, and in the spring and early summer of 1994 a program of massacres decimated the Republic of Rwanda. Although the killing was low-tech—performed largely by machete—it was carried out at dazzling speed: of an original population of about seven and a half million, at least 800,000 people were killed in just a hundred days. Rwandans often speak of a million deaths, and they may be right. The dead of Rwanda accumulated at nearly three times the rate of Jewish dead during the Holocaust. It was the most efficient mass killing since the atomic bombings of Hiroshima and Nagasaki.—Philip Gourevitch

Decimation is a Roman army invention.

Crucifixion originated with Persians, though Alexander the Great picked up on the practice, whence it was passed on to the enterprising Romans.

Force is as pitiless to the man who possesses it, or thinks he does, as it is to its victims; the second it crushes, the first it intoxicates.—Simone Weil

During my military career I was approached more than once to speechwrite. I always said no, unable to decide if writing for senior civilian or military leaders was pimping or whoring.

Shouldn't a requirement for the presidency be the ability to think and speak in paragraphs?

Who wrote for Jefferson?

Barry Bonds.

Roger Maris.

If you discover that some among them steal, you must punish them by cutting off nose and ears, for those are parts of the Body which cannot be concealed.—Christopher Columbus, 1494

In 1493, Europeans taste pineapple for the first time. Columbus is credited with discovering the fruit.

Duvalier, Papa and Baby too...

Columbus pointed out that Indians didn't use napkins and would give away their own things, as if they didn't believe in private property...

A T-shirt featuring mounted Comanche or Sioux. Printed above and below the image:

<div align="center">

HOMELAND SECURITY

———————————

Fighting Terrorism since 1492

</div>

Pineapple: Slang term for fragmentation grenade.

If you're in a war, instead of throwing a hand grenade at the enemy, throw one of those small pumpkins. Maybe it'll make everyone think how stupid war is, and while they are thinking, you can throw a real grenade at them.—Jack Handey

Again, thanks for the dud
hand grenade tossed at my feet
outside Chu Lai. I'm still
falling through its silence.
—Yusef Komunyakaa, from "Thanks"

Re: Handey
Buy the books! Resist frequenting the unauthorized websites. If you go

to his "official" website, however, you can vote as to whether there is a "real" Jack Handey. See <http://www.deepthoughtsbyjackhandey.com>. Do it. Treat yourself. Do it now.

According to Nicholas D. Kristof of the *New York Times*: The cost of one cruise missile would fund the building of 11 schools in Afghanistan. He also reports that the annual cost of posting 246 soldiers in-country would pay for a higher education plan for all of Afghanistan.

Genocide, after all, is an exercise in community building. A vigorous totalitarian order requires that the people be invested in the leaders' scheme, and while genocide may be the most perverse and ambitious means to this end, it is also the most comprehensive. In 1994, Rwanda was regarded in much of the rest of the world as the exemplary instance of the chaos and anarchy associated with collapsed states. In fact, the genocide was the product of order, authoritarianism, decades of modern political theorizing and indoctrination, and one of the most meticulously administered states in history. And strange as it may sound, the ideology—or what Rwandans call "the logic"—of genocide was promoted as a way not to create suffering but to alleviate it.—Philip Gourevitch

The specter of an absolute menace that requires absolute eradication binds leader and people in a hermetic utopian embrace, and the individual—always an annoyance to totality—ceases to exist.—Ibid.

And: *Without all that technology, the argument goes, the Germans couldn't have killed all those Jews. Yet it was the Germans, not the machinery, who did the killing. Rwanda's Hutu Power leaders understood this perfectly. If you could swing the people who would swing the machetes, technological underdevelopment was no obstacle to genocide.*—Ibid.

I'll tell you what war is about. You've got to kill people, and when you've killed enough they stop fighting.—Gen. Curtis E. LeMay

In Vietnam there were vaguer descriptions: *body count, attrition, free-fire zone*—name your comfortable label—but each a tallying of kills to show "progress."

You can't kill your way out of an insurgency.—Gen. David Petraeus

My father bought butter for himself and put the rest of us on a margarine diet. Was he cost-cutting or concerned for our health? Do you know?

By 1989, the total number of Vietnam veterans who died in violent accidents or by suicide after the war exceeded the total number of American soldiers who died during the actual war.

Military Glossary:
SNAFU (Situation Normal All Fucked Up)
Lifer
FUBAR (Fucked Up Beyond All Recognition)
Short-timer
FIGMO (Fuck It Got My Orders)
CLUSTERFUCK (Clusterfuck)

"Boy, I don't like you. You better move, you Communist motherfucker. I'm going to crawl up your ass and fuck you. I know the ragheads sent you to fuck up my Marine Corps."—Taped dialogue at Parris Island

Profanity, swearing, and verbal filth is discouraged. A person who must resort to profanity demonstrates his inability to verbally express himself in a socially acceptable fashion.—U.S. Marine Corps instructional manual

Knife Attack against a Sentry:
a. Be noiseless.
b. Your attack must be launched not less than five feet from your opponent.
c. Your attack should be immediate and from your opponent's rear.
d. Thrust your knife upward, into his kidney.
e. Place your free hand over your opponent's mouth and nose.
f. Withdraw your knife with a ripping motion.
g. Lift your opponent's head and slash his jugular vein.
—Ibid.

Profanity . . . is discouraged.

A slash rarely kills, however powerfully delivered, because the vitals are protected by the enemy's weapons, and also by his bones. A thrust going in two inches, however, can be mortal. You must penetrate the vitals to kill a man. Moreover, when a man is slashing, the right arm and side are left exposed. When thrusting, however, the body is covered, and the enemy is wounded before he realizes what has happened. So this method of fighting is especially favored by the Romans.—Roman army training manual

I am afeard there are few die well that die in battle.—Shakespeare, *Henry V*

Thich Quang Duc.

Pho.

War is God's way of teaching Americans geography.—Ambrose Bierce

Entr'acte

During the trek from Fairchild Hall (the academic building where I teach at the United States Air Force Academy) to Harmon Hall (the administrative building housing the three-star superintendent), it didn't occur to me that the general hadn't digested the point of the Holocaust Art Show. What would a Holocaust show be about if not the obscenity of war, the inhumanity of intentional degradation, the systematic slaughter of fellow humans? But: What the general said he *saw* was "naked people" (pronounced "neeked peeple"), which was not what he *wanted* the United States Air Force Academy to stand for.

Stand for?

The general was serious, tall and gaunt. In his tailored uniform, he made the case that rank depended almost entirely upon good posture and short hair. He uttered the word "ob-seen" as if he were a gruel-eating, humorless Lutheran direct from the Minnesota stage of *A Prairie Home Companion*. (Turns out he's from a neighboring state.) In any case, he discussed the art show (some 200 color drawings) as if it were a collection of discarded porn, then said he wanted the exhibit closed. We were all still standing: me, my boss (the department of English head), and the associate dean (both full-bird and senior colonels).

122

"Closed?" I said. "*Closed*?"

The three-star's executive officer (another colonel) was with him and doing his best to express and animate what he saw as the party-line outrage. He was pretty short, in his flight suit, and huffing, a sort of Renfield or Igor, a Marty Feldman deal.

"Just whose notion was this show?" he huffed, eager to place blame.

It was established that it had been *my* idea and it was established that he, *himself*, hadn't seen the show. But the general *had*, he told us for the general. We were all still standing.

"The last thing I need is for the *Gazette* [the local rag] to get a hold of this," said the three-star.

"A hold of what, sir? Art underscoring the consequences of war?"

"*Neeked peeple*," the ranking officer in the room said again.

"The show aroused you, sir?"—what I *wanted* to say, but didn't.

It's true the show contained disturbing images of people, many unclothed. I felt foolish explaining to a middle-aged man, who had fought in a war (Vietnam from the air), about the capture, abasement, and reduction of Jews, Poles, cripples, dissenting clergy, homosexuals, gypsies. William Schaff, in his gallery "Artist's Statement," had written: *I started with the basic, human figure. At our most basic, this is what we are, without possessions. I deeply believe that life is beautiful in all its possibilities and capabilities. So it seemed important to show that beauty being destroyed. Also, I recognize the level of discomfort people have with viewing the human figure, nude, in this way—naked really. I wanted that. I want the viewer to feel uncomfortable. There was no way I could have gotten the overall effect I was searching for with clothed figures. To strip the figures of their clothes strips them of a dignity we all recognize, and even when the viewer doesn't recognize that is what's happening, you can see they feel that humiliation in their not wanting to look at it. So many people seem to want to give these people back their clothes. When I used clothing in any of the images, it was generally to heighten that feel of humiliation. Considering what is happening to these people, they struggle to keep the clothes on they have, or are forced to expose themselves further. In showing the body, we see the beauty of the living, and all the potential it has, minus social identifiers we are used to. In showing the body destroyed we are forced to see what is lost, or being lost, and what is forever changed. I wanted to show that once such violence is imposed,*

123

we cannot do much to alter it. Without the text in hand, I walked the general through it: the artist's expressed ideas and motives. At one point, I said, "You know, sir, the academy is more than just an air force base with a big library. We're a university, too."

Renfield grunted.

I said, "Let's say you walked into the show and instead of broken victims—women and children—you saw a line of skinny men in striped pajamas behind, say, a few strands of barbed wire, a brick chimney in the background. Would that have made you feel better?"

"Yes," the general said.

The reason the general had stepped into the gallery in the first place was because he had just attended a session of the academy's annual National Character and Leadership Symposium. The session had been entitled "The Warrior Ethos."

I didn't think I could take the irony of what might have been discussed in that conference session, so I didn't ask.

When my boss and the associate dean spoke about the Holocaust show, the general stopped them by knowing he outranked them. He did everything except point to their shoulders and his. I, as a civilian, seemed to mildly perplex him.

The general returned to his fear of a report of the show in the newspaper.

"The *Gazette* was here yesterday," I told him.

Renfield glared his valet's glare.

"My guess is that it'll be positive," I said.

"What we have with this exhibit," my boss said, "is a chance to lead on an important fact of war—the atrocities that can occur, that *do*."

"Lead? I don't want to be on the leading edge of nothing," the general said. Then: "All I need is for some parent to call."

"Why is it so hard for you to understand we are a military institution?" the general's colonel asked. I think he was talking to me.

"Closing the exhibit will only bring attention to it," I said. "Think of the message. It's what the Gestapo would do." There: I'd said it: *Gestapo*.

The accord finally struck was that the gallery's doors were to be locked, and only opened to students in the presence of an instructor.

"But I want the glass covered, so passer-byers can't look in," the general said.

"Wrapped in brown paper?"

The general nodded and then so did his colonel.

"Tell you what," I said. "Maybe from now on, we should only bomb people who have their clothes on."

Renfield escorted me to the door. The man with three stars kept my two colonels. He had some things, he said, he wanted to tell them.

That night, at home, I reviewed the day. I'd made a copy of Schaff's "Artist's Statement," and read some more. Posing to himself the premise that most people's ingrained image of a Holocaust victim is an emaciated person, why had he chosen to depict healthier looking bodies?

I wanted to stay away from the images we are used to, because to most people my age such images mean very little, as sad as that is to say. Photographs of concentration camp prisoners—or even the piles of dead bodies—it's too easy for my generation to see these images, flinch and then move on. So I wanted to try and make the violation and the violence I felt more palpable. By starting with the model, someone that looked like you and me, and then showing the violence—an uncontrolled crush of paint or violent pen marks—I felt such an approach would create more impact than if I drew an image of, say, a Nazi soldier shooting someone. Movies and media have done much to take the power out of such an expected image. . . . How do you describe something you recognize is not describable? How do you show violation? Photography can be very gripping, but can also lose its effect over time, as it has, I believe, with my generation—such as is perhaps the case with images of piles of dead bodies or groups of thin people behind barbed wire.

At the time of the show, the artist is a shaved-head, body-tattooed, ear-ringed 26-year-old, and the three-star a 56-year-old fighter pilot who has dropped things on enemies' heads.

Here's the image that sticks:

In the general's office was his desk, large and cleared as a carrier deck. Telephone, pen set, and an oversized Snoopy Dog dressed out in full World War I regalia. Behind the three-star's desk a "Love Me" wall: plaques, awards, and photos of important people. Even outside dream, it is impossible not to imagine the general confiding in Snoopy, flying him off and onto the desk and around the room, rat-a-tat-tat-ing the Red Baron. *Boy, I guess we showed them, eh, Snoopy? Let's go home and change our uniforms, OK, pal?* For all I know, a grandkid gave the old man the stuffed animal, but, as I say, the image sticks.

When My Lai occurred, civilian reactions focused as much on the publicity of the massacre as on its occurrence. Readers wrote newspapers about the obscenity of depicting on front pages slain children and unclothed adults.

What to Know:
If you focus on the POWs in Hanoi, lauding their perseverance, honor, loyalty, and courage, then you have fashioned successfully a way in which to not deal with the harder questions of the U.S. presence in Southeast Asia . . .

A neighbor, a cardiologist, who smokes and rides a motorcycle without a helmet . . .

Are all barns red? Why?

You stayed away from me unless you were really curious about trouble.
—George Foreman

Silent Spring.

Convincing people to fight, and getting them to do it well, is one of the more essential and less noticed aspects of maintaining an armed force. Illusions must be created, and maintained, often unto death. Few individuals, once aware what combat is all about, want to spend any time at it.—James F. Dunnigan

No one who's been shot at retains the enthusiasm of the uninitiated.—Ibid.

Raw, unthinking courage is no match for firepower.—Ditto.

Abridgment:
Rage—Goddess, sing the rage of Peleus' son Achilles,

. . . 536 pages . . .

And so the Trojans buried Hector breaker of horses.

Gays in the Military:
Achilles
Leonidas of Sparta
Alexander the Great
Julius Caesar
Richard the Lionheart
Saladin
William of Orange
Frederick the Great
Lawrence of Arabia

Biological warfare began as early as the sixth century with poisoned wells—poison herbs were used, but so were animal and human corpses.

Don't be cruel.—Elvis

Fritz Haber, a Prussian Jew, directed the first gas attack in military history. He supervised the release of 150 tons of chlorine in 1915 across the fields of Flanders, killing British and French soldiers. He won a Nobel Prize for Chemistry in 1918. In time, he perfected Zyklon-B, originally put in use in low doses to de-louse German troops in the trenches of the Great War.

Haber's wife, distraught with her husband's chemical experiments, shot herself. The German government downplayed the suicide.

Stalin's second wife may have killed herself too. The son of his first wife tried to kill himself but botched it. Stalin criticized his son's marksmanship.

Ideas are more powerful than guns. We would not let our enemies have guns; why should we let them have ideas?—Iosif Vissarionovich Stalin

Chernobyl.

Chechnya.

An ice chunk four times the size of Manhattan has broken off a glacier in Greenland, hoisting danger to oil platforms and shipping lanes. (It was a Greenland iceberg that sank the Titanic.) The current iceberg contains enough fresh water to keep the Hudson River flowing for two years.

A U.S. congressman has suggested that the Petermann Glacier ice island might serve as a home for climate-change skeptics.

Fukushima Daiichi.

The Hayman Fire, my state's largest forest fire in recorded history, was started on June 8, 2002, by a federal forestry officer, Terry Barton, who claimed she was attempting to burn a letter from her estranged husband.

Five firefighters died, as did a local resident, who suffered a fatal asthma attack due to smoke inhalation.

Ann Dow (50 when she died) would have lived had Terry Barton not married?

Barton was sentenced to 12 years, but is out on probation after six. Besides the deaths, Barton is responsible for 138,000 acres burned, and the destruction of 133 homes and four times that number of outbuildings. U.S. District Judge Richard Matsch rejected the federal government's request that Barton be fined $14.7 million in restitution to pay for firefighting and restoration in the Pike National Forest. His public reasoning was that he didn't want to sentence Barton to poverty.

The Khmer Rouge, under Pol Pot, directed Cambodia for four years, during which time they murdered some 2 million Cambodian citizens, a full 25 percent of the nation's population. The Vietnamese invaded to stop that government and its slaughters.

Somebody thought Terry Barton had an extra $14 million lying about?

A Cambodian schoolteacher named Kang Kech Eav (code-named Duch) became head of the Tuol Sleng prison complex (code-named S-21).

*Duch oversaw a precise department of death. His guards dutifully pho-
tographed the prisoners upon arrival and photographed them at or near
death, whether their throats were slit, their bodies otherwise mutilated, or
so thin from torture and near starvation that they were beyond recogni-
tion. The photographs were part of the files to prove the enemies of the state
had been killed. Duch even set aside specific days for killing various types
of prisoners: one day the wives of "enemies"; another day the children; a
different day, factory workers.* —Elizabeth Becker

Sixteen thousand Cambodians perished in Tuol Sleng. There are 14
known survivors.

Duch was sentenced to 35 years in prison for his work as commander
of Tuol Sleng. The court ordered him to serve 19 years in prison, shav-
ing off 11 years for time served and five years more for being illegally
detained by a military court.

Can you be thought to have been illegally detained when the court, in
time, finds you guilty?

LeMay's five-month firebombing of Japan resulted in nearly as many
deaths as our own Civil War, which lasted four years, though LeMay
actually only bombed for four months over the five-month period.
Running out of ammunition following the March 1945 fire blitz, LeMay
had to wait four weeks for resupply.

Victory:
Assertive avoidance of war crime trials.

It takes 15,000 casualties to train a major general. —Ferdinand Foch

Boulder, Colorado, residents have so religiously exerted themselves to
conserve that the water authority has had to raise rates to cover expenses.

*What is an individual grief
but a flake in a storm?*
—Chase Twichell, from "The Shades of Grand Central"

My father escorted me to an icehouse beside a frozen lake near Belgrade, Montana. The ice from the lake, sawed by hand, was packed in stacks and sawdust, then hauled to people like my grandmother, who owned an "icebox" for refrigeration. My father informed that the ice, blocked and sawdusted, would last into summer. My father knew the owner of the icehouse, to whom he proudly introduced me.

His son: *Donnie.*

Note: Your refrigerator *makes* ice (and you can buy bottled water from Fiji, or Arkansas, or California).

The Greenland ice block, drifting toward Canada, cannot be stopped by humans or military equipment. Like all icebergs, nine-tenths of this giant calving rides beneath the surface and will run aground before its visible mass strikes the shore. The ice melt will be of a purity rivaling Fiji's.

The Japanese could figure this out. They certainly know how to paint cars. Is there anything like a white Toyota?

Mush yourself to the North or South Pole,
either icecap.
Chip from a glacier for your drink.
(You have brought, certainly, a tumbler?)
Add gin, room-temperature tonic. The air escaping the cleaving ice
is unpolluted. Give pause and ear
to the whisper—vaunted—of the ages:
a gassy tale 10,000 years told.
Inhale.

You could ask a question now, but what?
Is what you feel in this
unadministered place
a renunciation of your ambitions?
It may be you must admit to no
confusion here on this lidded retina

of the planet, to no sound of wind-
chattered flowers, grass.
Why is it you feel no sacrifice,
profundum, gain, loss?
Will you find it simpler mushing in
than out (as to and from a woman)?
Or is this about blunt waiting:
the shift, in the cold,
from one foot to the other,
grubbing for lore, instruction?
What is it you have for exchange:
fur, soy, clams, fruit?
a strong dog's lung?
some other untried church?
—"Scaling Ice"

road shoulder ice cracking like teeth or beetles . . .

Daughter, Waking in the Sierra Nevadas, Having Passed Her First Three Years in Sea-Level California: *That's a pile of dirt!*

The deep-throated growl of Harleys.

In the beginning, I'd write after the family was abed. Near 1 or 2 in the morning, I'd rub my eyes, strain to hear a knock at the door. In my mind, I'd rise to respond to a well-dressed adult on the porch: "Mr. Anderson, we understand there has been a literary event here tonight," but no. No knocks. No attired adults on the porch.

The Weed Wacker sound of Suzukis.

Sunni / Kurd.

Shiite / Kurd.

Sunni / Shiite.

We will always need stories to beat back our primal fears and remind us that there is something about our sad descent to the grave that is different from other animals. —T. C. Boyle

I remember Boyle's first published story: "Heart of a Champion." In this story, Lassie falls for a horny coyote that has attacked Timmy. Lassie deserts the blond-haired boy to follow her new love. Timmy, pinned beneath a log, drowns when the dam breaks and there is no rescue.

I wrongly remembered Lassie's downfall as a syphilitic Rin Tin Tin, no coyote.

How to Start a Story:
What to know about pain is how little we do to deserve it, how simple it is to give, how hard to lose. I'm a plumber. I dig for what's wrong. I should know. —Frederick Busch, "Widow Water"

What to Know:
The first thing to go is your legs, then your reflexes, then your friends.
—Willie Pep (1922–2006), champion boxer

What I Cannot Hear My Father Say:
"Use your *friendly* voice."

Willie Pep's nonfighting name was Guglielmo Papaleo. He fought 241 times, winning all but 12.

My parents did not know they needed a shredder. Did yours?

As an amateur boxer, I fought 17 fights, winning all but the last. Denny Miller hit me with punches I did not see. I got up once. The second time, I sat on the canvas, unwilling to move. Then, so there would be no confusion, I removed the gloves.

Eddy Lockett was our boxing coach. He was a baker who fought professionally, did his roadwork at 2 A.M. He taught us the rudiments in

the basement of our church. We had a couple of bags to hit, and each other. He made us wear mouthguards, but we had no headgear. He said not to hit each other in the balls. Eddy's preschool boy had a glass eye. He gouged out his eye, atop a chair, playing with a toilet plunger in a churning washing machine. Eddy's bakery lasted longer than his boxing career, but he died early of cancer. He taught us to pivot off the right toe when we threw a cross. "Supply pain" was his mantra. When I sat on the canvas to end my last fight, he tossed me a towel once the ref had counted, the count slowed to give me the option to get up.

He put me down almost immediately, and when I got up I was terribly afraid. I was tight and I could not breathe. It felt like he was hitting me in the face with a ball-peen hammer. It felt like he was busting light bulbs in my face. . . . I was convinced that his gloves were loaded, and a wave of self-pity ran through me.—Thom Jones, "The Pugilist at Rest"

Manny Pacquiao.

How to Write about War's Dark Core:
If a body is what you want,
then here is bone and gristle and flesh.
Here is the clavicle-snapped wish,
the aorta's opened valves, the leap
thought makes at the synaptic gap.
Here is the adrenaline rush you crave,
that inexorable flight, that insane puncture
into heat and blood. And I dare you to finish
what you've started. Because here, Bullet,
here is where I complete the word you bring
hissing through the air, here is where I moan
the barrel's cold esophagus, triggering
my tongue's explosives for the rifling I have
inside of me, each twist of the round
spun deeper, because here, Bullet,
here is where the world ends, every time.
—Brian Turner, "Here, Bullet"

Brian Turner wrote the poem in Iraq, folding the paper into a Ziploc bag, to carry in his breast pocket until his combat tour concluded, eight months ahead.

If I believe that everyone has the right to choose the manner of her own self-destruction, why do I wish my wife would stop smoking?

Here, Bullet: If you call something by its right name, like a dog, it will come?

Everyone has a plan until I hit them.—Mike Tyson

What makes more sense: Monroe or Lewinsky?

Birds remind him of fast hands, back when he
was no opponent, but took the number-two guy
twelve rounds and almost won. Should have. Did, many
said—and not just handlers.
—Jeffrey Skinner, from "Closed-Head Wounds"

An alcoholic woman in our neighborhood was rumored to strip to stand naked in her picture window, so I and Eddie Turner and George Lorango skulked, awaiting an appearance—a premiere—that never panned out.

Twitter / Tweet / Twitature.

Someone has tweeted the unabridged *Moby-Dick*, 140 characters at a time?

How to Close a Love Poem:
(i do not know what it is about you that closes
and opens; only something in me understands
the voice of your eyes is deeper than all roses)
nobody, not even the rain, has such small hands
—Edward Estlin Cummings, from "somewhere i have never travelled, gladly beyond"

When I write, I feel like an armless, legless man with a crayon in his mouth.—Kurt Vonnegut

Japanese Death Poems:
> *Death poems*
> *are mere delusion—*
> *death is death.*
> —Toko, 1795, at age 86

> *Spitting blood*
> *clears up reality*
> *and dream alike.*
> —Sunao, 1926, at age 39

> *Cherry blossoms fall*
> *on a half-eaten*
> *dumpling.*
> —Saruo, 1923, at age 63

I know a man who refers to his children as *those people*.

My father assumed I would own a truck, and for a short while I did, a Japanese model my father would have disapproved of. *Flimsy*, he might have said, when he meant *disloyal*. I resisted telling him about driving my truck into Pittsburgh, where a big man, crossing at the light, brought his fist down on the hood (leaving a dent), snarling, *Buy 'Merican!* This was 30 years ago, when a Nissan was a Datsun and its metal thin. I stayed in the Datsun, afraid the big man would brain me with his thermos.

The thermos appeared as if it would survive a fall from scaffolding.

He was a Republican, he said one week. Which meant to him gold bullion and gushing smokestacks and cars you hired a wetback to polish twice a month.—Lee K. Abbott, "The Talk Talked between Worms"

The right-wingers in Colorado have mounted resistance to Christo's

plan to drape the Arkansas River with fabric. The gist of their resistance is that this "art" is meddling with God's nature. And this despite the fact that the installation is temporary.

"Like tenting a tree."

"Putting a skirt on a tiger."

Jim Palmer (Hall of Fame pitcher) on Luck:
Sometimes you throw a great pitch and they hit it. Sometimes you throw a bad pitch and get away with it.

Edsel.

Yugo.

Gremlin.

Pinto.

We live in a country where one president is condemned for lying about sex and another is hardly chastened for supplying misleading reasons to go to war.

Neither Studs Terkel nor Joe DiMaggio ever possessed a driver's license.

Is it true that Nixon met with insiders to discuss assassinating *Washington Post* reporter Jack Anderson, whose despicable habit was exposing truth?

The United States Marine Corps *Guidebook of Essential Subjects* suggests that should you have to react to a nuclear explosion you *Drop flat on your stomach with your feet toward the explosion, close your eyes, place your hands under your body, and put your head down.*

Divorce will teach everything you need to know about selective memory.

If you were that close to a nuclear explosion, wouldn't you run toward it with your mouth open?

Graffito:
Save The Earth We Need Someplace To Boogie

So they have available now the Jesus Toaster™ that burns the imprint of Jesus onto your bread. Do you have this toaster?

Jesus has appeared as well on bagels, cheese sandwiches, potato chips, and as a sweet potato.

Are the buttons at crosswalks you're invited to push to stop traffic actually connected to something?

2010. There are two wars going on and in America everyone's Netflix still arrives on time . . .

I've a 40-year-old colleague who is like a 12-year-old who can buy beer. Do you have a friend like that?

How there is for every man some one scene, some one adventure, some one picture that is the image of his secret life, for wisdom first speaks images.—William Butler Yeats

Dialysis.

What is art, but surprise, then inevitability? Puffed with yearning.

If temporality were held to be invalidating, then nothing real ever succeeds.—John Updike

We should declare war on Vietnam. . . . We could pave the whole country and put parking stripes on it, and still be home by Christmas.
—Ronald Reagan, 1965

Even if a submarine should work by a miracle, it will never be used. No country in this world would ever use such a vicious and petty form of warfare.—William Henderson, British admiral, 1914

Your chances of dying in the Civil War were 1 in 15; in Vietnam 1 in 185.

2,100,000 people died during the siege of Stalingrad.

Richard Jordan Gatling, who gave us the world's first effective machine gun, was trained as a physician.

I call your attack a massacre, you call my resistance treachery. One of us may be lying, but one of us may lie dying. If I die, your word, "treachery," is almost as important as my wound, since you alone survive to make meaning of my death. War is a contest of injuries and of interpretation.—Jill Lepore

Henry Heimlich.

December 7th is memorialized as the day the Japanese bombed Pearl Harbor. August 6th is not memorialized as the day the Americans bombed Hiroshima. The Japanese killed outright 2,400 soldiers. The Americans killed 70,000 to 80,000 people, mostly civilians. After that atomic blast another 100,000 died from complications.

We weren't in My Lai to kill human beings, really. We were there to kill ideology that is carried by—I don't know. Pawns. Blobs. Pieces of flesh, and I wasn't in My Lai to destroy intelligent men. I was there to destroy an intangible idea.—Lt. William L. Calley

Deaths from 9/11:
Americans on American soil: 3,000, give or take.
Iraqis and Afghans on Iraqi and Afghan soil: 100,000, give or take.

How many photography shows entitled "Shadows and Light"?

On Three-Dimensional Art:
Sculpture is what you bump into when you back up to see a painting.
—Barnett Newman

The Dentist Who Says: *You might feel a little pinch.*

Dateline Manila: The Philippine House of Representatives has approved a bill criminalizing the improper singing of the country's national anthem. Any personal touches, slow singing, or incorrect beats or cadence are among possible infractions. Fines and jail time, up to two years, are among the punishments.

Entr'acte
During the 1980s I was running a marathon a year, training nonstop. One winter, on a blustery day—iced streets—a friend and I were running indoors on the U.S. Air Force Academy track. Some race-walkers from the U.S. Olympic Training Center were there too. My friend and I were clipping along at a seven-minute-mile pace, the pace at which I ran races—races in which I'd finish top third. When the walkers caught and passed us, I slowed, pulled up, and left the track. I showered, then walked to the library, where in those pre-Google days I looked up records for race-walking the 5 and 10K. Sure enough, both times were faster than I'd ever run them.

The ocean is a desert with its life underground and a perfect disguise above . . .—America, from "A Horse with No Name"

Bruce Wayne.

Fifth game of the World Series, Detroit, Michigan, 1968:
The same year Robert Kennedy and Dr. King are murdered, and Vietnam is at its height, out walks the blind Puerto Rican with his guide dog Trudy and his guitar. Feliciano's stylized version of the national anthem draws confounding criticism. Veterans, watching the series on TV, reportedly throw shoes and other objects at the on-screen artist.

When I was a kid I wondered how young Jack dealt with the giant's body after chopping down the beanstalk—decay, drinking water, cholera? No wait: I still wonder.

Though he lost twice to the Cardinals' Bob Gibson in the World Series, Denny McLain carded 31 victories during the 1968 season and was named as the AL's MVP and Cy Young winner.

See no evil, hear no evil, speak no evil. Whose idea was it to use the monkeys?

Never try to teach a pig to sing; it wastes your time and it annoys the pig.—Robert Heinlein

Denny McLain, the last 30-game winner of the twentieth century, spent the second half of his life in and out of prison: racketeering, gambling, cocaine, money laundering, embezzlement. The mysterious foot injury that disabled McLain for the last part of the 1967 season has been reported as the consequence of a mobster bringing a heel down on Denny's toes because of an unpaid bookmaking debt.

The human language is like a cracked kettle on which we beat out a tune for a dancing bear, when we hope with our music to move the stars.
—Gustave Flaubert

Fee, Fi, Fo, Fum.

Turns out that during the Nuremberg Tribunals, the United States was conducting medical experiments on Guatemalan male prisoners (in Guatemala), infecting them with syphilis by providing syphilitic prostitutes or, in the interest of efficiency, applying syphilis-ridden cotton to intentionally lacerated appendages, or by injecting the prisoners' spines with "syphilitic-mixtures"—all overseen by Dr. John Cutler of the U.S. Public Health Service. Following Guatemala, Cutler involved himself in the earlier-started-but-ongoing Tuskegee Study.

Cyberbullying.

The mythology of POWs still being held in Vietnam—a thriving industry selling flags and T-shirts.

Tell the truth, but understand that it is not necessarily what happened.
—Flannery O'Connor

When a writer is born into a family, that family is finished.
—Czeslaw Milosz

Week before last I went to Wesleyan and read "A Good Man is Hard to Find." After it I went to one of the classes where I was asked questions. There were a couple of young teachers there, and one of them, an earnest type, started asking the questions. "Miss O'Connor," he said, "why is The Misfit's hat black?" I said most countrymen in Georgia wore black hats. Then he said, "Miss O'Connor, The Misfit represents Christ does he not?" "He does not," I said. He looked crushed. "Well, Miss O'Connor," he said, "what is the significance of The Misfit's hat?" I said it was to cover his head, and after that he left me alone.—Flannery O'Connor, in a letter to Dr. Ted R. Spivey

And:
In most English classes the short story has become a kind of literary specimen to be dissected. Every time a story of mine appears in a Freshman anthology, I have a vision of it, with its little organs laid open, like a frog in a bottle.

Wallace Stevens suggesting art resists the intelligence . . . almost successfully?

Entr'acte
So: Tales of mountain men—Jim Bridger, Kit Carson, Jedediah Smith, Hugh Glass, John Colter—informed my Rocky Mountain youth. Hugh Glass, savaged by a grizzly—leg broken and claw-raked to expose ribs and scalp—crawled 100 miles, then floated the Cheyenne River on a makeshift raft to Fort Kiowa, 200 miles from where the bear had surprised him. It took Glass two months to crawl, then hobble to the

141

river. Glass had killed the bear with his knife, unable to effectively fire his rifle when the she-bear surprised him.

John Colter had been captured by the Blackfeet (a Canadian and Montanan tribe), who then, for sport, stripped him of his clothes and weapons and footwear. The Blackfeet then motioned him off, granting Colter a head start before beginning a sporting pursuit. Colter outlasted the racing warriors, with the exception of one, to whom he finally turned to kill with the brave's own spear. When he came to a river, Colter dove in to hide beneath a pile of logs until the straggling warriors and those on horseback finally quit the chase. Colter, having eluded the Blackfeet, then walked 200 miles to the nearest fort. To top off his career, John Colter is labeled the first white man to behold Yellowstone. The Colter story was one my father would tell each summer we made our trek to the national park. Even as a teenager, I wasn't bored by the tale. I thought about Colter's bare feet as he outsped the warriors.

Jim Bridger was 17 when he and an older trapper abandoned the mauled Hugh Glass, carting off Glass's weapons and gear. It had seemed reasonable to Bridger and the trapper that Glass would die, but it was the thought of revenge that fueled Hugh Glass's 200-mile trek to safety. Two years passed before Glass managed to track down Bridger. He had meant to kill the boy, but did not, given Bridger's age. Glass found the older trapper, but passed on that murder too, as the old man had joined the U.S. Army, making it a federal offense to kill him. The young Bridger went on to plot major routes through the Rockies and to discover the Great Salt Lake.

Watching the moon landing in 1969, it dawned on me that those white-suited men on the moon were in contact with civilization in a way my mountain men had never been. From 239,000 miles, we monitored Neil Armstrong's blood pressure and pulse. Few grizzlies or Blackfeet on the moon, light or dark side. *Radio contact.* And this surely: Armstrong had all the Tang he could drink.

You write a story because statement is insufficient.

My mother taught us to make hot Tang drinks. She had us add (dissolv-

ing in) some form of gelatin, good for our hair and nails, though that wasn't why I drank the doctored drink. I drained the hot cup because its contents were what I was told a spaceman craved.

Time to kill? Time is what we are.

> Estragon: *Was I long asleep?*
> Vladimir: *I don't know.*
>
> Estragon: *Why don't we hang ourselves?*
> Vladimir: *With what?*
>
> Estragon: *I can't go on like this.*
> Vladimir: *That's what you think.*
> —Samuel Beckett, *Waiting for Godot*

There has got to be some mystery in art, as in life, as to what is going on, and why...

Deepwater Horizon.

A melody is heard, played upon a flute. It is small and fine, telling of grass and trees and the horizon. The curtain rises. Before us the Salesman's house...
.......................................
Linda: *I made the last payment on the house today. Today, dear. And there'll be nobody home. We're free and clear. We're free... We're free...*
—Arthur Miller, *Death of a Salesman*

Blackwater.

Cruelest Deception:
Amnesia: for not to know who you were is to not know who to be.

The untranslatable thought must be the most precise. Yet words are not the end of thought, they are where it begins.—Jane Hirshfield

Number of Boeing 747s that could be constructed from the aluminum cans discarded by U.S. airlines: 58.

*Un*friend.

Pat Tillman.

Writers don't write so English teachers can concoct assignments.

I personally heard Ollie North say (at a Strategic Studies off-site in the Blue Ridge Mountains): "I know it's immoral, but is it illegal?" He was wearing Levis and a flannel shirt.

When I was a kid what we termed *Mongoloid* is what folks these days term *Down syndrome*. Mongoloid has become an offensive term (maybe it always was?) but has its origin in anthropology, as it is a reference to a major human racial classification distinguished by the physical characteristics—such as eyes that feature pronounced epicanthic folds, and prominent cheekbones—of the people of central and eastern Asia. That is, *Mongoloid*: characteristic of or resembling a Mongol.

In the town where I live, there is an annual "Buddy Walk." What we witness is, in a word, a parade of those with Down syndrome (along with their families and friends, leashed dogs, and caretakers). The parade, of course, has its own brand of sweetness, the featured participants enthusiastic and cheerful. *And look*: Lots of identical T-shirts and skyward balloons that have been lost hold of, the balloons' owners gaping up, stunned. *And this*: It is impossible not to note the difference between an afflicted 3-year-old wearing glasses and, say, a crew-cutted 63-year-old rumbling forward. These wide-girthed oldsters (that is, my age) are trailed by parents 20 years their senior, smiling kindly or appearing drained, beyond respite, having so remitted their own adult lives.

Epicanthus:
A fold of skin extending vertically over the inner angle of the eye: characteristic of Mongolian peoples and a congenital anomaly among other races.

Were I an actor of the method sort who required an image to work from for "sadness," I could do worse than call to mind a man with Down syndrome I saw each day on my drive to work along the Falls River Turnpike, on my way into the capital of this nation, Washington, DC. Rain or shine, the wide-faced citizen would be standing always beside—*outside*—the covered bus stop. When it rained, water coursed down his face from his lank, black hair. On his raised face was bewilderment, a look of abandonment and betrayal.

Over beer, in the Blue Ridge Mountains, Ollie complained about congressmen who complained about North's use of taxpayers' money to install a security fence around his home and to buy snow tires for the family car. I fully believe that North fully believed he had put his family at risk with his government work—his selling of arms to Iran to finance Nicaragua's Contras, etc.—and that he had places he needed to get to, despite unforeseen storms. Ollie North appeared on the Jerry Springer Show during its first season.

Down syndrome is a genetic disorder causing lifelong mental retardation, developmental delays and other problems. Down syndrome varies in severity, so developmental problems range from moderate to serious. Down syndrome is the most common genetic cause of severe learning disabilities in children, occurring in one in every 700 to 800 infants.
—MayoClinic.com

Time magazine's "Top 10 Worst Renditions of the National Anthem" doesn't mention Jose Feliciano. It does mention, though, Rosanne Barr, Carl Lewis, and Hillary Clinton.

How to Silence Yappers You Find beside You on a Plane:
Look, I know you mean well, but I've just been released from prison, and am not yet comfortable around random people.

What We Talk about When We Talk about Taliban Talking:
The officer said to Nadir, "Brother, tell your sister not to go to school. Otherwise we will kill her." The man was serious. Recently, there had been a chilling message broadcast on the radio in Mazar: "There are only

*two places for an Afghan woman," the radio announcer had said. "In the
husband's home. And in the graveyard."* —Doug Stanton

Iran-Contra.

Qala-i-Jangi.

When an Englishman speaks with his accent, do you assume he's brilliant? And when Australians yap do you assume they sound like frat boys, poachers, opal miners, surfers?

In the United States, on record, is the fact that 11 blind citizens have bowled perfect "300" games.

Entr'acte

Two years before he died, my brother, James Arthur Anderson II, asked to visit. He was on his way to Alamosa, Colorado (in the San Luis Valley, bordering the Great Sand Dunes, and Jack Dempsey's birthplace), and, as he put it, "Your house is in the way." Fifteen years earlier, I'd told my brother I never wanted to see him again, and that if I did see him—big brother that I was—I would bestow *hurt.* My suggestion of providential violence was hollow noise as Jimmie was seven years younger, half a foot taller, and savvy as a burned snake. My brother had been in the army, broken horses, brawled in bars, and had survived in a Canadian prison (after working over that off-duty Royal Canadian Mounted Policeman with a bat). He'd also stolen, then squandered, my father's life savings, which was the reason I'd told him to stay away.

When I pulled in from work, Jimmie was parked, facing the wrong way, beside the sidewalk in front of my house. He was dismantling his truck, engine parts on the asphalt and grass. When he saw me, he stepped down from his chrome front bumper. He performed a fairly competent about-face and showed me his hands. They were dirty, black. For a minute I realized how long it had been since I wielded a ratcheting wrench, a double jack, an axe. My shoes were impractical: Corfam—a polished plastic that made your feet sweat. Jimmie wore boots with thick soles, probably steel-toed, oil-resistant. I was in polyester uniform, two years from retirement after 22 years of active military service. Viet-

146

nam came and went and I'd forgotten to muster out. I'd kept meaning to, but the air force had sent me to university twice for advanced degrees, and I was, and had been, teaching English at the United States Air Force Academy. My attempt to dodge Vietnam as a foot soldier had led somehow to my dream profession—teaching college. Jimmie gave me the once over, then saluted. "*Colonel*," he said. We embraced. Jimmie had been a private in the army, dishonorably discharged for serial AWOL.

Though it's not accurate, my recollection is that my brother had his truck's engine, block and all, out and set on the ground. I not only see the engine outside the truck, I can hear it running. I can picture my dead brother adjusting the idle.

On the street side of my sidewalk, on a strip of lawn, were a half-dozen full-grown trees: pin oak and Russian elm. Leaned against each trunk was at least one rifle, a couple of them scoped. In my mind's eye, I also see ammunition and the knife in his boot that Jimmie would show me later. In the street, he was stripped to the waist. He was scarred: stomach, ribs, back, fingers. I pointed to one nasty mark. *Bullet*, he said. Then he touched another: *box cutter*. I knew something about ribs and horses, and I brought that up. He said something to the effect that only men were sneakier than livestock. A couple of kids coasted by on their bikes. I asked if the rifles were loaded. Jimmie: *A lot of good they'd be if they weren't.*

I went into the house to change. Ellen was making supper. "So, that's Jimmie," she said. "We've talked. He's happy to see you." Then: "We should eat on the porch." Ellen had never met Jimmie as she and I had, at that time, been married three years.

As I recall Ellen's words, I realize it was full summer when Jimmie visited. The trees leafed out and the grass green. The sky blue and light until 9 P.M. The sound of timed sprinklers doing their work.

Jimmie reassembled his truck, stowed his weapons, and showered. When he came out to eat, his hands were cleaner, his hair combed. His T-shirt was new. It was black cotton that had never been washed, and featured a furling American flag. He had the shirt tucked in. When he turned his back on purpose, dropped out in white was: *Try to Burn THIS ONE, Asshole!*

When he turned to sit, the chain hooked to his keys and oversize wallet chimed. "I knew you'd like it," he said. "*Colonel*."

147

Jimmie didn't stop on his way back north to Idaho, where he lived with his wife and guns. The shotgun he stole from my father was the one he chose to shoot himself in the head, on that day his second shipment of morphine patches had arrived. As I told you a hundred pages back: When Jimmie was released from prison, he rode a horse from Alberta to Sante Fe. Who do you know who has done that?—"AWOL"

Five times more people are learning English in China, than there are people in England.

In my reading life, no one has written better sex than Updike, though my favorite insight of John's occurred when he characterized the Bee Gees as white guys who figured out how to sing like black women . . .

There are 1,198,500,000 people alive now in China. To get a feel for what this means, simply take yourself—in all your singularity, importance, complexity, and love—and multiply by 1,198,500,000. See? Nothing to it.—Annie Dillard

As of 2010, seven times the number of American dead in Iraq and Afghanistan have died in Mexico in its drug wars.

For years my father played Santa for the children at the annual church Christmas party. He so loved the role that he finally bought his own suit—an extravagant mail-order outfit. The following year, the church elders informed my father that they were no longer in need of his services.

In any war there are people who disappear.—Gen. Leopoldo Galtieri, Argentina, 1982; qtd. in Gustafson

Q: Is organized religion making things better or worse?
A: The fact that an atheist has never set himself up in a duck blind to shoot at people exiting an abortion clinic sort of gives you that answer, doesn't it?—Robert Dubac

Slobodan Milosovic.

What No Man Wants to Hear as He Walks in the Door:
On Dr. Phil today...

Anita Hill.

The Oprah Book Club.

Let them hate, so long as they fear.—Caligula

The 33 miners (trapped more than 2,300 feet underground in Chile) for the initial 18 days survived on two mouthfuls of tuna and half a cup of milk every two days. Once they were discovered living (a note being passed to the surface up the first small bore hole to reach them), food, medicine, and correspondence flowed for the next 50 days until the large bore hole was completed and the miners raised (one at a time) in a capsule the width of a small man's shoulders. An early request from one of the trapped Chileans was for a photo of the sun.

With the leaves all gone you can see the branches real good . . .

All the time I was growing up in Butte, the Anaconda Company was king, owning the town and all its folk. Before Chile nationalized its own copper mines, Anaconda made a fortune mining in the Andes. When Anaconda first opened the mines, they employed, of course, local natives. An early problem was that once the natives had earned a paycheck, they quit working. As it turned out, the natives' lives (and needs) were simple—most had a single dream, and when they were able to purchase that dream they abandoned mining. The Anaconda Company solved the problem by providing the miners with Sears, Roebuck and Co. catalogs.

Tariq Aziz, the international face of Saddam's regime, sentenced to 15 years in prison, has been subsequently sentenced to hang by an Iraqi court. Aziz is reputed to have saluted the telephone whenever Saddam called.

As of 2010, the United States is spending (for military assistance alone) $100 billion a year in Afghanistan—this for a country with a GDP of $14 billion. At least $1 billion a year is being transferred out of Afghanistan by top government officials and other well-connected Afghans. Karzai has lashed out against investigations of this sort.

Believe me, if Hitler were to say I should shoot my mother, I would do it and be proud of his confidence.—Heinrich Himmler, qtd. in Ackerman

This existence of imaginative literature within a culture signifies that all of that culture's cards are not on the table; they may, in fact, be nowhere in sight. The desire to get them on the table, under control and neatly arranged, prompts the telling and retelling of tales. It is the very function of the imagination to wonder and question; the culture in which there are no conflicts needs no wonder. By telling, literature is also asking. Through written dramatization, an act of communication, other members of the culture are invited to participate in the attempt to resolve conflicts. Literature, then, is something very much like a cry for help; the worse the conflicts, the more they are repeated in tale after tale.—A. Carl Bredahl Jr.

Like all men, I tell a hundred lies a day.—Vance Bourjaily

Crime doesn't pay?

Love conquers all?

Virtue is rewarded?

Great minds think alike?

Your dog doesn't bite?

They paved paradise and put up a parking lot . . .—Joni Mitchell, from "Big Yellow Taxi"

Visual Pollution:
What can be seen belongs to everyone.

Shadrach, Meshach, and Abednego.

Atchison, Topeka, and Santa Fe.

Lennon, McGuire, Andrews.

Bosh, Wade, James

How to Start a Novel:
My story begins, like everything else, on the beach. Beaches are the same the world over, you peel down, then you peel off; they serve you up raw meat, dark meat, or flesh nicely basted in olive oil. A strip of sun and sand where the sex is alert, the mind is numb. The beach in question, one of the best, is near where Sunset Boulevard meets the sea. I don't mean to be ironic. California is that way naturally. It's hard to do malice to California, but this particular strip might have been in Acapulco, or down in Rio, or along the Riviera. If it's world brotherhood you want, go to the beach. If you like parallels, the beach is where we came in, and where we'll go out. Having crawled from the sea, we're now crawling back into it. That solution of salt in the blood is calling us home. And in a mammary age, what better place to compensate for an unsuckled childhood?—Wright Morris

You've got to have something to eat and a little love in your life before you can hold still for any damn body's sermon on how to behave.
—Billie Holiday

How to Start a Memoir:
In our family, as far as we are concerned, we were born and what happened before that is myth. Go back two generations and the names and lives of our forebears vanish into the common grass. All we could get out of Mother was that her grandfather had once taken a horse to Dublin; and sometimes in my father's expansive histories, his grandfather had owned trawlers in Hull, but when an abashed regard for fact, uncommon in my father, touched him in his eighties, he told us that this ancestor, a decayed seaman, was last seen gutting herrings at a bench in the fish market of that city.—V. S. Pritchett

Mom and Pop were just a couple of kids when they got married. He was eighteen, she was sixteen and I was three. —Billie Holiday

Joni Mitchell's favorite singers: Edith Piaf and Billie Holiday.

Three things that cannot be long hidden: the sun, the moon, the truth. —Buddha

In 2001, the Taliban exploded two ancient, monumental statues of Buddha as a righteous blow against heresy.

I have always depended on the kindness of strangers. —Blanche, *A Streetcar Named Desire*

The Buddhas had silently served for 1,500 years. The male Buddha was 174 feet tall.

In 2010, Kathleen Lorie Folden, 56, drove 690 miles from Kalispell, Montana, to Loveland, Colorado, to destroy a work of art that, in her mind, disrespected Jesus. The weapon she brought was a crowbar. After, shirt emblazoned with the words "Tougher than Nails," Folden informed reporters, "God is real."

The Hungarian religious fanatic who in madness, screaming *I am Jesus Christ!*, scaled a marble balustrade to attack Michelangelo's *Pietà* with a car mechanic's hammer, cleaving the Madonna's nose, breaking her left arm (milk-white marble fingers snapping as the left hand struck the floor) in a Vatican basilica . . .

Heinrich Heine, in the 1820s, understood that people who burn books will, in time, burn people.

Re: Ali:
Joe Frazier, sitting in his corner, nearly blinded from blows, sobbing, *I hit him with shots what woulda knocked down the walls of a city.* Frazier hadn't been able to see for two rounds. For six minutes, he'd absorbed

blindly all Ali threw. Still, Frazier had wanted to fight the final round, the 15th.

Re: Frazier:
Muhammad Ali admitted to have almost quit in the 10th: *It was like death.*

Both fighters were hospitalized, after this, their third and finest encounter.

Technically the loser of two of the three fights, [Frazier] seems not to understand that they ennobled him as much as they did Ali . . . that the only way we know of Ali's greatness is because of Frazier's equivalent greatness, that in the end there was no real difference between the two of them as fighters, and when sports fans and historians think back, they will think of the fights as classics, with no identifiable winner or loser. These are men who, like it or not, have become prisoners of each other and those three nights.—David Halberstam

Joe Frazier would come out smoking. If you hit him, he liked it. If you knocked him down, you only made him mad.—George Foreman

Daughter's Description of South Africa, to Where She Has Relocated:
A cross between San Diego and Jamaica, with better birds.

How to Explain Wine:
You could spend the rest of your life tasting wine and still not exhaust its variations, each bottle a little ecosystem of grapes and soils and weather, yeast and bacteria, barrels of wood from trees with their own soil and weather, the variables cross-multiplying until each glassful approaches a singularity, a moment in time on earth.—Ellen Ullman

<div align="center">

HOW'S MY DRIVING?
CALL 1-800-EAT SHIT

</div>

Kristallnacht.

After half a day of babysitting grandchildren and surveying the play-room mess, I said: "What's this crap?" "*Crap*"—the 5-year-old announced—"Papa, is a *bad* word." Then: "There are three *bad* words: *fuck*, *crap*, and *hell*."

Just north of the mountain town where I live is a wolf preserve, from where, of a moonlit night, you can hear old songs of lamentation and yearning. The *Canis lupus* can bite through bone, creating a bite pressure of up to 1,500 pounds per square inch. A human bite has been tested to an average force of 200 pounds.

Domesticated dogs, no doubt, came about as a consequence of wolves following human hunters to take advantage of abandoned carcasses. Some years passed before dogs began guarding sheep and cattle instead of eating them.

It's just a job. Grass grows, birds fly, waves pound the sand. I beat people up.—Muhammad Ali

Gul Mudin.

And: *I ain't got no quarrel with the Vietcong. No Vietcong ever called me Nigger.*

Dementia pugilistica: *The condition, which occurs in boxers who have suffered repeated blows to the head, manifests as dementia, or declining mental ability, problems with memory, and Parkinsonism, or tremors and lack of coordination. It can also cause speech problems and an unsteady gait.*

Over two-thirds of Vietnam's population has been born since the Fall of Saigon.

The sump pumps that were preventing mine waters from entering the Berkeley Pit were turned off on Earth Day, 1982. The Pit remains the nation's largest Superfund site.

Aung San Suu Kyi.

Fantasy Football—how does that work?

Fewer people are wearing watches as time is omnipresent (on your computer screen, your cell phone, your car dashboard, your microwave oven).

Kalid Sheik Mohammed.

And Then There Were Four:
Erie, Huron-Michigan, Ontario, Superior. Michigan and Huron are hydrologically a single lake.

Rocky Flats, a former nuclear plant (1952–92) located on a windy plateau 16 miles northwest of Denver, is a new refuge in the U.S. Fish and Wildlife Refuge System. At Rocky Flats, plutonium triggers for atomic bombs were fashioned.

Korengal Valley.

Historically, Rocky Flats site activities resulted in the contamination of surface environmental media with actinides, including isotopes of americium, plutonium, and uranium.—Todd and Sattelberg

How to Cite:
Todd, A. S. and Sattelberg, R. M. (2005), Actinides in deer tissues at the rocky flats environmental technology site. Integrated Environmental Assessment and Management, 1:391–396. doi: 10.1002/ieam.5630010408.

surface environmental media?

Under the refuge conservation plan, the U.S. Fish and Wildlife Service will develop a limited public hunting program. A study of radioactivity in deer on the Rocky Flats site, done in 2004 by scientists with the Service, found "minimal human risk" from eating deer meat taken at the Flats.

155

Dust in the wind...

Americium is produced by bombarding plutonium-239, an isotope of plutonium, with high-energy neutrons. Americium is used in smoke detectors and can be used as a portable source of gamma rays.

Plutonium possesses a half-life of 24,400 years. When plutonium (in minuscule amounts) is taken into the body, the result is generally cancer, damaged immunity, genetic abnormalities . . .

A gamma-ray burst from space could wipe out all living species on the planet Earth at any time, with no warning, and destroy the ozone layer in the process. A gamma-ray burst is the consequence of supernova explosions, star deaths, etc.

The U.S. Fish and Wildlife Service, which manages 550 wildlife refuges nationwide, has agreed to post signs explaining the history of Rocky Flats as that area is turned into recreational public land.

During the EPA investigation, one building at Rocky Flats was dubbed the most dangerous structure in the country by the U.S. Energy Department.

A solemn consideration, when I enter a great city by night, that every one of those darkly clustered houses encloses its own secret; that every room in every one of them encloses its own secret; that every beating heart in the hundreds of thousands of breasts there, is, in some of its imaginings, a secret to the heart nearest it! Something of the awfulness, even of Death itself, is referable to this.—Charles Dickens

With new rules in place, nearly $4 billion was spent on the 2010 midterm elections. That's enough to buy 333,333 families of four enough groceries for a year.

Or: Send 28,571 people to Harvard for four years . . .

. . . just to watch them is to feel again that hitching in the groin,
 that filling of the heart,
the old, sore heart, the battered, foundered, faithful heart, snort-
 ing again, stamping in its stall.
—C. K. Williams, from "Love"

She called my name once. I didn't even know she knew it.
—Robert Penn Warren, from "True Love"

After Chernobyl, deer radioactivity north of Snasa, Norway, averaged about 70,000 Bq/kilo, with a few deer as high as 137,000 Bq/kilo. Deer from the Vilhelmina area in northern Sweden averaged 12,000 Bq/kilo after post-Chernobyl slaughters. During the same period, over two-thirds of deer slaughtered in Kautokeino, Norway, were under the 6,000 Bq/kilo limit set by the Norwegian government and could be sold. Reindeer pastures in Finland were affected only very slightly by Chernobyl fallout and there were no restrictions on the sale of Finnish deer. The Swedish government radioactivity level for salable foodstuffs is considerably lower than Norway's, set as it is at 300 Bq/kilo.

The becquerel (Bq) is a unit of radioactivity. One Bq is defined as the activity of a quantity of radioactive material in which one nucleus decays per second. The becquerel is named for Henri Becquerel, who shared a Nobel Prize with Pierre and Marie Curie for their work in discovering radioactivity.

Is it possible that the imagination is not separate from memory, but a faculty thereof?

There are known knowns; there are things we know we know. We also know there are known unknowns; that is to say we know there are some things we do not know. But there are also unknown unknowns—the ones we don't know we don't know.—Donald Rumsfeld

Alexander the Great hauled *The Iliad* with him on campaign.

Suicide bombers are easy to spot. They give out all kinds of tell-tale signs.
Mostly because they're nervous. By definition they're all first-timers.
—Lee Child

Aretha Franklin, Rosemary Clooney, and Mary Travers (of Peter, Paul, and Mary) before they got fat . . .

Alexander led his first military force at 16. Then upon his father's death commanded his conquering army until age 33, at which time he died in the palace of Nebuchadnezzar II of Babylon. During his military career Alexander survived a cleaver slash to the head, a sword blow to the thigh, a catapult missile in the chest, an arrow through the leg, a stone to the head and neck, a dart in the shoulder, an arrow in the ankle, and an arrow in the lungs. There is speculation that he died of alcohol poisoning or a relapse of malaria contracted 13 years earlier in 336 B.C.

The Heartbreak of Psoriasis.

George W. Bush in flight gear aboard the carrier USS *Abraham Lincoln.*

When hemorrhoids were called piles . . .

I am tired of fighting. Our chiefs are killed. Looking Glass is dead. Toohul-
hulsote is dead. The old men are all dead. It is the young men who say
yes or no. He who led the young men is dead.
 It is cold and we have no blankets. The little children are freezing to
death. My people, some of them, have run away to the hills and have no
blankets, no food. No one knows where they are—perhaps freezing to
death. I want to have time to look for my children and see how many I
can find. Maybe I shall find them among the dead.
 Hear me, my chiefs. I am tired. My heart is sick and sad. From where
the sun now stands, I will fight no more forever.—Chief Joseph of the
Nez Percé

Teddy Roosevelt required his U.S. military officers to cover 50 miles on foot in 20 hours to maintain their commissions.

I am not afraid of an army of lions led by a sheep; I am afraid of an army of sheep led by a lion.—Alexander the Great

Do not expect:
When bombs fall on people
they will be thankful;
that bombs will tilt the scales
the way the experts presume.

Expect:
Every war contains traces of all the others.
—Jason Armagost, from "These Four Archaic Truths
and Martial Virtues"

How to Write Understatement:
We were in a garden at Mons. Young Buckley came in with his patrol from across the river. The first German I saw climbed up over the garden wall. We waited till he got one leg over and then potted him. He had so much equipment on and looked awfully surprised and fell down into the garden. Then three more came over further down the wall. We shot them. They all came just like that.—Ernest Hemingway

A snake disappearing is often more memorable than one completely visible.—Mark Irwin

The number of humble-bees in any district depends in a great measure upon the number of field-mice, which destroy their combs and nests; and Colonel Newman, who has long attended to the habits of humble-bees, believes that "more than two-thirds of them are thus destroyed all over England." Now the number of mice is largely dependent, as every one knows, on the number of cats; and Colonel Newman says, "Near villages and small towns I have found the nests of humble-bees more numerous than elsewhere, which I attribute to the number of cats that destroy the mice." Hence it is quite credible that the presence of a feline animal in large numbers in a district might determine, through the intervention first of mice and then of bees, the frequency of certain flowers in that district!—Charles Darwin

Global Economy.

Yoknapatawpha.

Entr'acte

Have you passed a kidney stone? It's like crucifixion. OK, that's hyperbole, but it is how I saw it at the time. It's even how I see it now, because when you have passed the stone (it took me three hours) it feels like resurrection. I passed the stone, stopped vomiting, and my body temperature dropped six degrees. Having borne the ordeal, my first fear was that kidney stones might travel in pairs, like snakes.

You can no more win a war than you can win an earthquake.
—Jeannette Rankin

There Were Five:
Chico, Harpo, Groucho, Gummo, Zeppo.

Entr'acte

Following a week in Tomkins County Hospital, I was home with my colostomy, 42 years old, feeling worked over and sporting a shit bag on my belly. I was feeling sorry for myself, and sad. When I pissed that morning and it looked like blood, I paused before I flushed the toilet. I debated showing the stained water to Ellen, then shoved the lever. *"Christ!"* I said, expelling air. I emptied my chest: *"Fuck!"* I waited until I had to pee again, then showed Ellen. She called the surgeon, who set up an immediate consult with a urologist. As soon as I reached the hospital, I was on my back, stirruped up. I could see the doctor's green-capped head between my legs, his face and beard masked. He revealed a forearm's length of stainless steel, a rod he told me was a camera. "We're just going to take a look," he said. Then: *"You're going to feel a little pressure."* He said this quickly, then ducked his head. The pressure was instantaneous and breathtaking. I puffed like a woman in labor. If there were curves in there—and it seemed there should be—the rod

160

was straightening them out. "So," he said, unseen, "red? *Lipstick*-red? *tomato*-red? *cherry*?," sounding a little chirpy to me. "Yes," I puffed, "*red. Beet*-red." Suddenly: The doctor's face. He jerked off the mask. "*Beet?*" he said. "Did you say *beet?*" "I did," I said. I half-expected Groucho Marx, his cigar, and the duck. "*Beets*," I said. "Ellen steamed a batch. From the *Farmer's Market*." The doc withdrew the rod, that thrust up, as if independently, like a wand ashining. I could see the beam at its tip. "*Fiber Optics*," the doctor pronounced, like I'd pronounced *Farmer's Market*. The urologist passed the lit wand to a nurse. "Everything looked fine in there," he said. "Big bowl of beets," he said. "Big bowl," I said.

Owning a cashmere sweater is like owning a little dog, a thin dog, a *fake* dog. If you're going to have a dog, then get a dog. If you are going to wear a sweater, then wear one . . .

Buffalo Bill's
defunct
 who used to
 ride a watersmooth-silver
 stallion
and break onetwothreefourfive pigeonsjustlikethat
 Jesus
he was a handsome man
 and what i want to know is
how do you like your blueeyed boy
Mister Death
—Edward Estlin Cummings

Robert Allen Zimmerman.

Mozart played all the notes; Basie played some of them. Which is why jazz is more imaginative than classical music. Which is why, for me, Ellington fails, opting for both forms at once.

Elin Nordegren.

Yamaha makes pianos *and* motorcycles?

1909. Geronimo dies, at 90, of pneumonia, still a prisoner, at Fort Sill, Oklahoma.

Tracking the seven dwarfs: two S's, two D's, three emotions: Sleepy and Sneezy; Dopey and Doc; Happy, Bashful, and Grumpy.

The clock talked loud. I threw it away, it scared me what it talked.
—Tillie Olsen

Surely you can't be serious . . .
I am serious, and don't call me Shirley.
—Leslie Nielsen, *Airplane.*

Olga Khokhlova.

Ferris Bueller.

December:
My parents both died in December; my first wife's birthday is in December, Pearl Harbor, all disasters. Though my sister was born on Christmas, my parents celebrated her birthday each year on June 25th—they didn't think she should have to compete with Jesus.

Raoul Wallenberg.

Patna, India:
An argument over sacrificing goats during a Hindu festival honoring the goddess Durga triggered a stampede that killed 10 people in a packed temple. More than 40,000 people had taken some 30,000 goats to be butchered at the temple. Supplicants were vying with one another to get their goats sacrificed when a shoving argument broke out with a butcher. Four women and six men died in the ensuing stampede. Liquor is purported to be involved.

The goddess Durga represents the power of the Supreme Being that

preserves moral order and righteousness. Durga, also called Divine Mother, protects mankind from evil and misery by destroying evil forces such as selfishness, jealousy, prejudice, hatred, anger, and ego.

Nat King Cole starring as W. C. Handy in the *Father of the Blues* . . .

Scientists in the United Kingdom compared the hands of 1,500 prostate-cancer patients and 3,000 healthy men. Those whose index finger was longer than their ring finger were 33 percent less likely to develop the disease. Did you just check? How did that turn out?

Not all nonsmokers escape . . .

Ambien.

A bear's breath each Spring . . .

Noxema.

Outside of a dog, a book is a man's best friend. Inside of a dog, it's too dark to read.—Groucho Marx

No great dependence is to be placed on the eagerness of young soldiers for action, for the prospect of fighting is agreeable to those who are strangers to it.—Vegetius, Roman military writer, fourth century A.D.

How to Name a Trailer Park:
Emerald Acres, Shady Haven, The Grove, Swan Meadow, Foxridge Farms, Holiday Hills, Cherokee Cluster, Canterbury, Skyline, Harmony Homes, Redwood Estates, Lago Vista, Golden Terrace, Villa West, Pueblo Grande, Hillcrest, Green Valley, Tourmaline . . .

Tourmaline: a hard, variously colored crystalline borosilicate mineral. Use: electronics, optics, gems.

Valley? Check the creek bottoms, the vistas near the landfill, mine-shafts, and other declivities inviting hail, flood, locusts, frogs, thistle,

tornadoes. . . . It's there you'll find Green Valley, The Townes, Loch Lomond, Shangri-La . . .

. . . nothing works like clockwork, not even clocks.
—Robert Urquhart, "Toy"

I did nothing but explore the world with my hands and learn the name of every object that I touched; and the more I handled things and learned their names and uses, the more joyous and confident grew my sense of kinship with the rest of the world.—Helen Keller

His art is eccentricity, his aim
How not to hit the mark he seems to aim at,

His passion how to avoid the obvious,
His technique how to vary the avoidance.

The others throw to be comprehended. He
Throws to be a moment misunderstood.
—Robert Francis, from "Pitcher"

I tink I twy sometin diffunt. I tink I twy
sometin exciting like wacing cawrs. Sometin to make
my heart beat at a difwent wate.
But den you just can't quit being sometin like
SPIDERMAN.
You SPIDERMAN for life. Fowever. I can't even
buin my suit. It won't buin. It's fwame wesistent.
So maybe dat's youwr pwoblem too, who knows.
Maybe dat's da whole pwoblem wif evwytin.
Nobody can buin der suits, dey all fwame wesistent . . .
—Jim Hall, from "Maybe Dats Your Pwoblem Too"

Memory (the deliberate act of remembering) is a form of willed creation. It is not an effort to find out the way it really was—that is research. The point is to dwell on the way it appeared and why it appeared in that particular way.—Toni Morrison

164

If I were to remember different things, I should be someone else.
—N. Scott Momaday

Though thought of as quintessentially American, Charlie Chaplin was British-born. Charlie once entered a Charlie Chaplin look-alike contest, in which he placed third.

Steamboat Willie.

1927. *Time* magazine's first "Man of the Year" was Charles Lindberg: *Lucky Lindy*.

The rage of the disesteemed is personally fruitless, but it is also absolutely inevitable; this rage, so generally discounted, so little understood, even among the people whose daily bread it is, is one of the things that makes history.—James Baldwin

Orval Faubus.

Hubble.

A Reminder:
In 1925, John Scopes was found guilty for teaching the theory of evolution. He was fined $100 and relieved from his teaching duties. William Jennings Bryan, who spoke for the prosecution, died of a stroke within a week after the trial. Scopes, for his part after the trial, attended the University of Chicago, where he studied geology. A committee of scientists and intellectuals, headed by a former president of Stanford, had raised the funds for Scopes's further education. The Tennessee law prohibiting the teaching in public schools of theories contrary to accepted interpretation of the biblical account of human creation was not repealed until 1967.

Speechless animals . . . are limited to single-stage transactions. They wander, as we do, searching for facts to fit their sparser stock of hypotheses, but when the receptor meets its match, this is only a single thud. Without

language, the energy that is encoiled, springlike, inside information can only be used once.—Lewis Thomas

The most basic barrier was language itself. Very few of the Americans in Iraq, whether soldiers or diplomats or newspaper reporters, could speak more than a few words of Arabic. A remarkable number of them didn't even have translators. That meant for many Iraqis, the typical nineteen-year-old army corporal from South Dakota was not a youthful innocent carrying America's goodwill, he was a terrifying combination of firepower and ignorance.—Dexter Filkins

What does much more to distinguish our specific human from non-human memory is our social existence, and the technological facility which has created a world in which memories are transcribed onto papyrus, wax tablets, paper or electronic screens; that is, a world of artificial memory. It is artificial memory which means that whereas all living species have a past, only humans have a history.—Stephen Rose

1918. Two years before my father's birth, 650,000 Americans died from influenza, four times the number of U.S. troops who died in World War I. A feature of this flu was that its victim could awaken feeling well, fall ill by noon, and be dead by nightfall.

The Triangle Shirtwaist Co. paid its female garment workers $1.50 for their 72-hour workweek. On March 25, 1911, 146 of these workers died when fire swept the top floors of a building in Greenwich Village. Many of the women leapt to their deaths, as the exit doors were locked during work hours.

Core temperatures of the Twin Towers flirted with 2000°F, not enough to melt steel, but more than enough to soften steel for collapse. Steel melts at 2750°F. Iron requires 45 additional degrees.

To cause the face to appear in a mass of flame make use of the following: mix together thoroughly petroleum, lard, mutton tallow and quick lime. Distill this over a charcoal fire, and the liquid which results can be burned on the face without harm.—Harry Houdini

When I was a kid, I worried that we lived in a house without a sidewalk. For the past five years I've lived in a loft in the city. There are sidewalks . . . complete with street musicians, panhandlers, spit, dog shit, gum.

Added Bonuses:
Garbage trucks in the morning; sirens; buses; cooped-up dogs who leave their deposits, yapping.

Dandy Don Meredith.

The Graveyard of Empires.

Iwo Jima: an 8-square-mile volcanic island south of Japan.

How to Start a Story:
I visited my friend and we talked about shoes instead of about dying. I wanted to talk about dying, but she's the one who's dying and she wanted to talk about shoes. —Rochelle Distelheim, "The Kiss-Me-Quick"

Three of the six men who raised the Stars and Stripes on Mount Suri-bachi were killed before the end of the island battle.

How to Write about Flash Fiction:
I was on a bus to Washington, D.C. Two days I'd been traveling and I was tired, tired, tired. The woman sitting next to me, a German with a ticket good for anywhere, never stopped yakking. I understood little of what she said but what I did understand led me to believe that she was utterly deranged.

She finally took a breather when we hit Richmond. It was late at night. The bus threaded its way through dismal streets toward the bus station. We rounded a corner and there beneath a streetlight stood a white man and a black woman. The woman wore a yellow dress and held a baby. Her head was thrown back in laughter. The man was red-haired, rough-looking, and naked to the waist. His skin seemed luminous. He was grin-ning at the woman, who watched him closely even as she laughed. Broken glass glittered at their feet.

There is something between them, something in the instant itself, that

makes me sit up and stare. What is it, what's going on here? Why can't I ever forget them? Tell me, for God's sake, but make it snappy—I'm tired, and the bus is picking up speed, and the lunatic beside me is getting ready to say something.—Tobias Wolff

Mogadishu.

DADT.

We are always what we were; we know ourselves—to the degree that knowledge of the self is possible—through our ever-growing past. . . . Memory gives us a double perspective: not only does the past inform the present, but the present informs the past. In other words, the understanding of our present selves that memory provides us is capable of returning the gift, enabling us to know our earlier selves in a manner that eluded us then.—James McConkey

I am certain of nothing but the Holiness of the Heart's affections and the Truth of the Imagination.—John Keats

Distortion was a compromise, something in its very nature disingenuous, the product of a conflict between thought and feeling . . .—Sigmund Freud

Ted Kaczynski.

Mark Zuckerberg.

1913. Suffrage March on Washington.

How to Proffer Advice:
Never put whiskey into hot water bottle crossing borders of dry states or countries. Rubber will spoil taste. Never make love with pants on. Beer on whiskey, very risky. Whiskey on beer, never fear. Never eat apples, peaches, pears, etc. while drinking whiskey except with long French-style dinners, terminating with fruit. Other viands have mollifying effect. Never sleep in moonlight. Known by scientists to induce madness. Should bed stand beside window on clear night draw shades before retiring. Never hold cigar

at right-angles to fingers. Hayseed. Hold cigar at diagonal. Remove band or not as you prefer. Never wear red necktie. Provide light snorts for ladies if entertaining. Effects of harder stuff on frail sex sometimes disastrous. Bathe in cold water every morning. Painful but exhilarating. Also reduces horniness. Have haircut once a week. Wear dark clothes after 6 P.M. Eat fresh fish for breakfast when available. Avoid kneeling in unheated stone churches. Ecclesiastical dampness causes prematurely gray hair. Fear tastes like a rusty knife and do not let her into your house. Courage tastes of blood. Stand up straight. Relish the love of a gentle woman. Trust in the Lord. —John Cheever*

Every gun that is made, every warship launched, every rocket fired, signifies—in the final sense—a theft from those who hunger and are not fed, those who are cold and are not clothed. The world in arms is not spending money alone. It is spending the sweat of its laborers, the genius of its scientists, the hopes of its children. —President Dwight David Eisenhower, April 16, 1953

Entr'acte

Sonny Gillespie was a kid we marked a half-breed, the sort of character Charles Bronson might have played in those days' films. We knew Sonny was part Indian, but not what tribe, and we knew his old man was Mexican. In some way, this mix was enough from which to deport our harassing. We knew Sonny because he went to our church, and came in his crappy clothes to our scout meetings and, for a while, to our boxing class. At least a dozen kids lived in his house. My father knew Sonny's father, because they both worked in the mines. My crew and I'd chase Sonny down and tie him with ropes, all the time calling him "Chief" or "Mex," settling, finally, on "Squaw." Once Georgie Lorango brought electrician's tape and we taped Sonny to an aspen. We always left him trussed up wheresoever we nabbed him. One time, we lowered him roped into a window well at the church. It was so deep that even if he had been able to unrope himself, he couldn't have climbed out of the well unassisted. Sonny wasn't a bad boy, and certainly no bully. In boxing class, we'd all try to match up against him because he wouldn't hit back, and you could whale away without fear or resistance. All Sonny

169

ever really worked on was how to outrun us, and in time he was able to do that. Over a couple of summers, he lengthened without gaining weight and began to quite easily outpace us. Confident, he once stopped to chuck rocks, and even after one caught Georgie in the neck and then Eddie in the chest we couldn't catch him. We called Sonny *Sonny*, but I doubt now that this was his actual name. Despite the nearness of his home (with its dirty kids and cows and pigs and chickens and dogs, cats, sagging fenced pens and tin-roofed sloping house additions), Sonny seemed to disappear like the blacks I never saw at school, and Eddie and Georgie and I went on to high school without him. It's 50 years since I laid eyes on Squaw. When my father died I returned to Butte for the funeral. I walked out the backyard of the homestead and through the field (now fenced and grassed) toward where the Gillespie compound had stood but now housed concrete slabs and sewers for trailers that had either not arrived or had departed. The word *ignorance* floated by—and not the unknowing sort, which may be forgivable. It was a *knowing* ignorance, a belligerent and aggressive ignorance from which we had performed our work. Pathetic, really, and criminal. What I'd expected to experience standing in the field outside of what had been the Gillespie housing, I hardly know. What I felt was ransacked and tiny. If you know Sonny, have him call.

And so you wonder about child soldiers after mixing in fear, hunger, murder, dismemberment, drugs?

Do you believe the French electrician who today claims that Picasso's second wife forked over 271 works of art 40 years ago in appreciation of the electrician's work in wiring Picasso's villa for burglar alarms? The cache of work includes lithographs, portraits, watercolors, and sketches, as well as nine Cubist collages worth an estimated $56 million alone. For the moment the art is in the hands of the French police and the 71-year-old electrician has not been charged.

Charles Bronson was neither Indian nor Mexican, but one of 15 children of struggling Lithuanian immigrant parents in Pennsylvania. His father, too, was a miner, though of the coal-digging sort. After serving

in World War II, Bronson used the GI Bill to attend art school. In a breakthrough role he was cast as the half Irish/half Mexican gunslinger Bernardo O'Reilly in *The Magnificent Seven*.

First-World Issue:
People, several years into the Great Recession and $4 drinks, return to frequenting Starbucks. The term employed to explain this return is *austerity fatigue*.

Retail Signage:
Unattended children will be given espresso and a free kitten.

Charles Bronson's actual name is Karolis Bučinskis. He earned a Purple Heart in WWII as an aerial gunner on a B-29.

A neighbor's son, just back from Baghdad, will not eat falafel, in the manner of my uncle, who fought in the Pacific and refused to believe in Japanese barbers upon his move from Conrad, Montana, to San Diego in the early 50s.

Everyone understood the deal. The attack on the World Trade Center was an act of war. Despite the occasional chatter in the press about shoddy steel or substandard fireproofing, the towers were as well designed, built, and maintained as could have reasonably been expected in America in the late twentieth century. But the context had changed now. The towers fell because they were severely maimed and sprayed with burning jet fuel; they fell as any building will, no matter how resilient, if it is hit by the next bigger missile in the escalating progression of war. In retrospect, their greatest failing was so obvious that it hardly required discussion: the stairwells had been clustered too closely together, and their simultaneous destruction had trapped people above the impact zones, causing more than a thousand unnecessary deaths. This was an error that would have to be avoided in future designs. But there was no point in wishful thinking here. Civilians die in wars, and always will. —William Langewiesche

Chiclets.

Father Knows Best.

The powder that filled the 9/11 air, covering whatever remained or moved through it, consisted primarily of crushed concrete.

Betty Ong.

LGBT.

People who came to the site in those early days often had the same first sensation, of leaving the city and walking into a dream. Many also felt that they had stumbled into a war zone. "It's like something you'd see in the movies," people said. Probably so, but my own reaction was different when I first went in, soon after the attacks. After years of traveling through the back corners of the world, I had an unexpected sense not of the strangeness of this scene but of its familiarity. Wading through the debris on the streets, climbing through the newly torn landscapes, breathing in the mixture of smoke and dust, it was as if I'd wandered again into the special havoc that failing societies tend to visit upon themselves. This time they had visited it upon us. The message seemed to be "Here's a sample of our political science." I was impressed by how faithfully the effects had been reproduced on the ground.—Langewiesche

Alfred Kinsey.

Richie Havens.

Speaking of a 600,000-Ton, 110-Story Tower:
Still, if not exactly shrugging off the hit, the South Tower had absorbed it well: absent an earthquake or strong windstorm, the building would have remained standing indefinitely.
 But then, of course, there was the fire . . .
 The fire fed on wrecked office furniture, computers, carpets, and aircraft cargo, but primarily it fed on ordinary paper—an ample supply of the white sheets that were so much a part of the larger battlefield scene. Without that paper . . . experts believed, the fire might not have achieved the intensity necessary to weaken the steel beyond its critical threshold.

It would be simplifying things, but not by much, to conclude that it was
paperwork that brought the South Tower down.—Langewiesche

The tsunami waves caused by the eruption of Krakatoa were 120 feet
in height. Coral blocks weighing as much as 600 tons were thrown
ashore. In those 1883 Indonesian waters, the tsunami waves traveled
at calculated speeds of 300 mph. The sound of the initiating explosion
was heard 3,000 miles away.

On the door it says what to do to survive
But we were not born to survive
Only to live
—W. S. Merwin, from "The River of Bees"

Life is moments, day by day, not a chronometer or a contractual commit-
ment by God.—Edward Hoagland

You think
I am speaking in riddles. But I am not, for
The world means only itself.
—Robert Penn Warren, from "Riddle in the Garden"

It is common knowledge—isn't it?—that the prizes Alfred Nobel
funded, benefiting science, culture, and peace, were (and are) made
possible by his manufacture and sale of TNT?

It is forbidden to kill; therefore all murderers are punished unless they kill
in large numbers and to the sound of trumpets.—Voltaire

Frank S. Emi.

The Shadow Knows . . .

Megaton: a measure of explosive power (of an atomic weapon) equal
to that of one million tons of TNT.

"Castle/Bravo" (the largest nuclear weapon detonated by the United

States), set off at Bikini on February 28, 1954, produced twice the energy expected from 8 million tons of TNT—an explosion equivalent to some 15 million tons of TNT.

The world's most powerful hydrogen bomb was detonated on October 30, 1961, over Novaya Zemlya by the Soviet Union. The bomb had an explosive force of 58 megatons, or almost 6,000 times more powerful than the Hiroshima bomb. Dropped by an aircraft, and detonated 1,200 feet above the earth's surface, the Novaya Zemlya shock wave was so powerful, that it circled the planet three times, the mushroom cloud extending 38 miles into the atmosphere.

The Soviets labeled the experiment *Tsar Bomba*.

Alfred Nobel's father manufactured land mines.

The heft of truth.

2010. David Hockney's Pixelated Period:
The Pierre Berge-Yves St. Laurent Foundation in Paris is hosting Hockney's art that was created on an iPad and then e-mailed to the gallery. The Paris show consists of nonpaint paintings on luminous digital screens. One wall at the gallery is hung with 20 iPhones; a second wall carries 20 iPads. "You could print a Hockney e-mail, if you were lucky enough to get one," says the gallery coordinator, "but it would lose something in translation without that brilliant backlighting. The work only lives on these gadgets."

I've used dynamite (in the mines). What one stick, or six sticks, can do would shock you. Fifty-eight megatons?

The atomic bomb dropped on Hiroshima was .02 megatons, a tiny thing.

My father would often drop food off at the Gillespie compound, quietly, in the dark, though one or two of the dogs would raise enough fuss that Mr. Gillespie or a kid would come to the door to look. By then,

my father would be back crossing the field, away from the Gillespie setup that looked like a defunct fruit stand or petting zoo. My father never asked or forced me to deliver food bags, but would make me accompany him to *Safeway* or *Albertson's* to pester the produce managers for fruit or vegetables they were about to throw out. If rebuffed, my father would climb into the dumpsters himself to look. Once home, my father would clean the carrots or apples or turnips or spuds, washing and paring bruised or spoiled parts in order to bag his findings. His deliveries were fairly constant but would increase if the mines were on strike or there were layoffs. Whenever my father would score cases of vegetables or fruit he would actually can the food to preserve it and to deliver it in bottles—pickles, beets, peaches . . .

The man who does not read good books has no advantage over the man who cannot read them.—Mark Twain

It's not like anything
* they compare it to—*
the summer moon.
—Bashō (1644–94)

A tethered horse
* snow*
in both stirrups.
—Buson (1716–83)

The man pulling radishes
* pointed my way*
with a radish.
—Issa (1763–1827)

A poem is an event, not the record of an event.—Robert Lowell

mid-argument
wind chimes
we gave each other.
—Peter Newton

175

Twelve-year-olds suck ice
outside a shop hawking
fruit and child-size caskets.
—"Sao Paulo"

How to Write about Marriage:
Marriage is not
a house or even a tent.

it is before that, and colder:

the edge of the forest, the edge
of the desert
the unpainted stairs
at the back where we squat
outside, eating popcorn

the edge of the receding glacier

where painfully and with wonder
at having survived even
this far

we are learning to make fire.
—Margaret Atwood, "Habitation"

Entr'acte

Early in my air force career, I was stationed at a radar site in Alaska—Indian Mountain, Alaska. I panned for gold in the Indian River—thinking of my grandfather's Yukon—and found a few flecks that I stored with a pinch of black sand in an emptied prescription vial. If you shook the sand, the gold glittered through.

Morale at the site was low because our outdated equipment was nearly useless. We were to be tracking the Russian Bear in those Cold War-days. Our fear was that Russian bombers would over-fly us to the lower 48—toward our families and homes—and we'd never know. Our equipment was so obsolete that we seldom caught our own mail plane coming in. We'd be studying our screens when someone would open the door to say the mail plane had landed, as it did each week on

our unimproved, gravel runway, which upsloped at an 8-degree angle, straight into the side of a mountain. In the flight pubs, it read in bold print: *Successful go-around highly improbable!*

During winter, Indians would motor up the frozen river to our site to congregate at our "Club"—a designated room in our compound that we used as a bar. We had a record player, a couple of dartboards, a pool table. The camp cook would fry you a steak if the chow hall was closed and the fire crew took turns tending bar.

It was against federal law to sell unopened liquor to Indians, so we didn't. I was reminded why I'd been born in Montana: my grandfather, unsatisfied with his moonshine sales, started moving his hooch onto the Ute Reservation. The Feds caught wind of this and meant to snare him. Tipped off, Grandpa loaded my father and his sister and my grandmother into the Model T. They drove until they ran out of fuel in Butte.

We sold liquor-by-the-drink to our visitors, which *was* legal, no matter how many bottles it led to. Drunked up, the young Indians would kick-start their snowmobiles to drive home. Home was a fishing village on the Koyukuk—a primary northern tributary to the more famous Yukon.

There was an older Indian who, when he traveled, came by sled. When he finished drinking, he wouldn't mush home. No matter the weather, he would sleep with his dogs. At 4 or 5 in the morning, the dogs would wake the camp, yipping. The old Indian would toss them frozen fish, then head home. Some nights he would spend outside with his dogs, the temperatures would drop to 50 or 60 below.

In time, I asked why he didn't drive a snowmobile. He looked at me. "What are you going to do if your engine dies, eat the carburetor?"

The summer before I left Alaska, the old Indian walked me along the river to Gold Camp, five or six miles upstream. He'd hiked in from Koyukuk to visit. He'd brought two dogs and the fish to feed them. The huskies stayed within range, like sheepdogs.

On our way to the camp, we steered clear of the banked gravel and walked on tundra, which gave with our steps and released clouds of mosquitoes and gnats. I wore long sleeves and a cap with netting. When I sprayed my hands with repellent, the old Indian closed his mouth and covered his nose.

He had pointed out the dredged banks of the Indian River. He told

me about the hydraulic mining before the war. He meant, he said, "The World War: Number Two." He extended an arm to wave it across the screen of the sky. "Over-digging," he said, toeing the bleached gravel, which stretched out of sight, both banks. "Water mining strips living from earth. Pollutes watersheds. Kills fish."

In Gold Camp, the dredgers were rusted, bear had ransacked the cabins, and returning soldiers had had better offers in the lower states. We found swollen cans of tomatoes the bears had missed, old newspapers, and mattresses full of thin snakes and rodents. From the scat, we could see that even moose had sometimes sought shelter. The old Indian talked about gold and arsenic and spoiled water. He smelled like salmon.

Before we headed back to the radar site, we walked along the river. What I thought to be a glacier canopied the water at a bend. I asked how old the ice was.

"Gone by August," the Indian said.

The ice—blue as sky—towered above. We stood where the river tunneled through, tempted by the microclimate. Following us from the 22-hour summer sun, the mosquitoes and gnats joined black flies in the misty cool. It was as if we were standing inside a bell.

Because I attended graduate school late in my life, I felt often as if I'd awakened to find myself surrounded by youngish amateurs who'd purchased expensive and muscular Ski-Doos. These folk circled to talk torque and horsepower and to pretend intimacy with snow and killing weather. I felt like the old Indian who wanted privacy, safety, and to sleep with his dogs.

I once repeated his words in a graduate course where the students came each week to books—twentieth-century novels—with equipment: excavators, dredgers, powered tools.

I said, "Hydraulic mining strips living earth, pollutes watersheds, kills fish." And when no one understood: "You can ruin anything—even love—with too much of this." Then: "Tell me you love me. *Count* the ways. *Specify*. Provide five reasons in descending order as to why you love me. Tell me more." —from "Tell Me a Story"

Art is only a substitute while the beauty of life is still deficient.
—Piet Mondrian

But all they want to do
is tie the poem to a chair with rope
and torture a confession out of it.

They begin beating it with a hose
to find out what it really means.
—Billy Collins, from "Introduction to Poetry"

Cut a bird in search of song . . .

How to Write Disaster:
Down on the field they all had their faces turned up to the sky. They saw Whelan pop out of the cockpit. With his Martin-Baker seat-parachute rig strapped on, he looked like a little black geometric lump a mile and a half up in the blue. They watched him as he started dropping. Everyone waited for the parachute to open. They waited a few more seconds, and then they waited some more. The little shape was getting bigger and bigger and picking up tremendous speed. Then there came an unspeakable instant at which everyone on the field who knew anything about parachute jumps knew what was going to happen. Yet even for them it was an unearthly feeling, for no one had ever seen any such thing so close up, from start to finish, from what amounted to a grandstand seat. Now the shape was going so fast and coming so close it began to play tricks on the eyes. It seemed to stretch out. It became much bigger and hurtled toward them at a terrific speed, until they couldn't make out its actual outlines at all. Finally there was just a streaking black blur before their eyes, followed by what seemed like an explosion. Except that it was not an explosion; it was the tremendous crack *of Ted Whelan, his helmet, his pressure suit, and his seat-parachute rig smashing into the center of the runway, precisely on target, right in front of the crowd; an absolute bull's-eye. Ted Whelan had no doubt been alive until the instant of impact. He had had about thirty seconds to watch the Pax River base and the peninsula and Baltimore county and continental America and the entire comprehensible world rise up to smash him. When they lifted his body up off the concrete, it was like a sack of fertilizer.*—Tom Wolfe

179

Whatever weight is hung on a wheel, which weight will cause the motion of that wheel, there is no doubt that the center of that weight will come to rest under the center of that axis. And no instrument that human ingenuity can make, causing that axis to turn, will have power to do away with that effect. —Leonardo da Vinci

I paint what I want to see. —Philip Guston

After weeks of watching the roof leak
 I fixed it tonight
by moving a single board.
—Gary Snyder

Outside of town
the cows lay down
because they have always done so.
They have never pretended
that there was anywhere
to hide.
—Benjamin Busch, from "Storm Shutters"

Rick Nelson was one of the first artists that audiences both saw and heard at once. He performed a song at the end of segments of "The Adventures of Ozzie and Harriet." Because this rock 'n' roll music came at the conclusion of a family sitcom, it worked to speed that music to become more acceptable sooner. When *Life* magazine ran a cover story on Nelson, they coined the term "teenage idol."

How the Author Begins My Favorite Novella:
In our family, there was no clear line between religion and fly fishing. We lived at the junction of great trout rivers in western Montana, and our father was a Presbyterian minister and a fly fisherman who tied his own flies and taught others. He told us about Christ's disciples being fishermen, and were left to assume, as my brother and I did, that all first-class fishermen on the Sea of Galilee were fly fishermen and that John, the favorite, was a dry-fly fisherman. —Norman Maclean

How He Ends It:
I am haunted by waters.

It's all in the art, you get no credit for the living. —V. S. Pritchett

Key Strategy:
Do not assume that the trout will move great distances to the fly! Get
the Fly to the Trout! This means placing the fly at the right *depth* and
on the right *drift line.*

Kilgore Trout.

Life is no way to treat an animal. —Trout's epitaph

In *Good Measure*, poet Robert Morgan quotes poet Donald Hall: *Words
are the sensuous body of pleasure, but content is pain.* Morgan's interpre-
tation is to the point: *It is the carnality of language that gives pleasure,
but the vexation of meaning provides significance.*

In "Nail Bag," Robert Morgan recounts how settlers moving on would
burn their houses and barns, to retrieve the nails. At the new homestead
they'd reuse them:
*. . . Then took out the sack
of nails like slivers of crystal
that hammered right would summon
wilderness into new structure.
As though all husbandry and home
were carried in that charred handful
of iron stitches, blacksmithed chromosomes
that link distant generations.*

How to Write a Poem about a Carpenter's Tool:
*Shifty-eyed as an auctioneer, the bubble
hides quick. Every touch makes it overshoot
its lines. The nervous little fish
of emptiness backs, then rushes forward*

in the vein of elixir, hunting
high ground, hoping for the outlet
to burst into the open. No rest except
when aiming at the center of the sky
and at the center of the earth.
Put to sleep by accuracy.
—Robert Morgan, "Spirit Level"

Language is a skin: I rub my language against the other. It is as if I had
words instead of fingers, or fingers at the tip of my words. My language
trembles with desire.—Roland Barthes

What the Poet Knows:
A thought or opinion is not an image.

Of course, since the events I have begun by recording took place some
twenty years ago, I don't pretend those were the actual words we used.
Yet like Thucydides I was there, and like him I have made Mother, Father,
and myself speak not words we actually spoke but only such words as in
my opinion are reasonable and proper for us to have spoken on the occa-
sion. Just as poetry is more philosophic than history, so memory is more
rational than a tape recorder.—Thomas Rogers

Bad Jobs:
Computer salesman, security guard, eunuch.

No ideas but in things . . .

More than 1.5 million tons of steel, debris, and bodies were removed
from Ground Zero. In a place where 3,000 people died, only 18 were
recovered alive. During the first 10 months of recovery, a little over a
third of the remains were identified and only 293 could be thought of as
anywhere near whole bodies (mostly firemen whose clothing and gear
preserved them). The rest of the discovered 1200 victims were identified
from among some 20,000 body parts. The known but undiscovered
remains were burned, pulverized, or vaporized.

Remarkably, of the 50,000 workers at the World Trade Center, 95 percent of them escaped.

Most of the recovered steel from the Twin Towers has found its way through the canal in Panama to China and India.

Charles Ponzi.

I once built a Palestinian village with small milk cartons and glue and salt. It was for Sunday school and I won a prize—a flannel board on which to attach cut-out biblical figures at Christmas or Easter, to illustrate those stories.

Armed movements seek divine sanction and the messianic certitude of absolute truth. They do not need to get this from religions, as we usually think of religion, but a type of religion: Patriotism provides the blessing. Soldiers want at least the consolation of knowing that they risk being blown up by land mines for a greater glory, for a New World. Dissension, questioning of purpose, the exposure of war crimes carried out by those fighting on our behalf are dangerous to such beliefs. Dissidents who challenge the goodness of our cause, who question the gods of war, who pull back the curtains to expose the lie are usually silenced or ignored.
—Chris Hedges

Before conflicts begin, the first people silenced—often with violence— are not the nationalist leaders of the opposing ethnic or religious group, who are useful in that they serve to dump gasoline on the evolving conflict. Those voices within the ethnic group or the nation that question the state's lust and need for war are targeted. These dissidents are the most dangerous.—Ibid.

Webinar.

A *fungo* bat is used for fielding practice. It is lighter, longer, and thinner than an ordinary baseball bat, allowing a good hitter control to the extent that he can lead outfielders and make them run. One version

of the word's etymology is that some exhausted outfielders yelled *fuck you* in Italian to the Italian batter.

How Religion Can Work:
I know my ancestors preferred this sacred fear, which promised an eventual dividend in the beyond, to the never-ending and coldly unanswerable fear of the elements, disease, ruin, war. All fears could be consolidated into that one conveniently central fear, which permitted some alleviation through good works and mortification of the flesh. It ruled the seasons, explained chance, accounted for anomalies.—Luc Sante

What is Wall Street but Las Vegas without the pools and hotels?

If you are careful enough, nothing good or bad will ever happen to you . . .

Sonny and Cher, Tom and Jerry, Ben and Jerry, Nixon and Ford, Procter and Gamble, Mantle and Maris, Bob and Ray, Curds and Whey, Laurel and Hardy, George and Gracie, Malone and Stockton, Ozzie and Harriet, Yin and Yang, Ike and Tina, Warp and Woof, Fred and Ginger, Jan and Dean, Jordan and Pippen, Rocky and Bullwinkle, Kobe and Shaq, the Lone Ranger and Tonto, Bush and Quayle, Strawberries and Cream, Bonnie and Clyde, Nixon and Spiro, Sturm und Drang, Jekyll and Hyde, Cisco and Pancho, Roy and Dale, Click and Clack, Fibber McGee and Molly, Simon and Garfunkel, Don and Phil, Me & Bobby McGee, Franny and Zooey, Janus . . .

Philco.

Studebaker.

DeSoto.

The apparition of these faces in the crowd;
petals on a wet, black bough.
—Ezra Pound, "In a Station of the Metro"

In those days of cigarette glamour, LSMFT stood for *Lucky Strike Means Fine Tobacco*, which we, in elementary school, altered to *Loose Straps Mean Floppy Tits.*

And this we came across and learned by heart:
When the frost is on the pumpkin
That's no time for dickie dunkin'
But when the weather's hot and sticky
Oh, that's the time for dunkin' dickie

Sing-songing that ditty together made us feel mature, almost bearded.

Which Reminds Me, in My Adulthood, of My First Writing Mentor's Essential Conception:
Literary critics know all the positions, but haven't ever been laid.
—Alfred Kern

Wildroot.

Strontium-90.

Chromium-6.

How to Title a Country Song:
How Can I Miss You If You Won't Go Away?
Don't Know Whether to Kill Myself or Go Bowling
If I Said You Had a Beautiful Body, Would You Hold It against Me?
Still Miss You Baby, but My Aim's Gettin' Better
I Got Tears in My Ears from Lying on My Back Crying on My Pillow
 over You
If I Had Shot You When I Wanted to, I'd Be Out by Now
I've Been Roped and Throwed by Jesus in the Holy Ghost Corral
Why Have You Left the One You Left Me For?
Drop Kick Me Jesus through the Goal Posts of Life
You're the Reason Our Kids Are So Ugly

Eavesdropping:
I lost weight, cut and highlighted my hair, took up yoga, absorbed Russian,
and he wanted to know why I left him "out of the blue"....

Overheard a Colorado cattleman—a recognized pioneering sort in his
nineties—responding to a question as to whether he broke his casted
leg by falling from a horse. "It's like fucking niggers," he explained, "you
do it, but you don't yap about it."

An original use of the word *bolt* was to describe, as a noun, the arrow
used in a crossbow. It wasn't much of a slide to lightning *bolt* or *bolt*
your food, *bolt* from the room, even *bolt* the door which seems to in-
corporate the word as both noun *and* verb.

Buñuel.

. . . the substance of things hoped for, the evidence of things not seen.

Peter Parker.

Arafat.

Let us attend to the details of what is inevitable until it becomes mean-
ingful.—Jonathan Bishop, responding to lines from Emerson's essay
"Spiritual Laws"

Who Gets by on Shortened Names:
Emerson, Snead, Marino, Cézanne, Pollock, Bono, Moses, Ali, Gandhi,
Flaubert, Koufax, Cher, Eisenhower, Dempsey, Camus, Gretzky, Tyson,
Clemente, Lincoln, Elway, Mandela, Stallone, Elvis, Marilyn, Tiger,
Oprah, Ronnie, Barack, Ringo, Rush, LeBron, Hillary, Magic, W, FDR,
MLK, Basie, Papa, Faulkner, Satchmo . . .

Pelé's real name is Edison "Edson" Arantes do Nascimento.

First rule of bartending: Don't leave your knife on the bar.
—Thomas Vargish

Words That Feel like What They Are:
bougainvillea, wavy, serene, pontificate, rococo, whipsaw, gibberish, bigwig, haircut, rambunctious, killjoy, palaver, coagulate, chatter, heartbeat, springboard, lightbulb, warehouse, bicker, potlicker, piggyback, flummoxed, unruly, carefree, layaway, gravestone, unearth, unspent, unsalved, windfall, kerfuffle, blowhard, lickspittle, lollygag, dilly-dally, ruckus, mouthwash, wordsmith, nippy, nerve-wracking, turnkey, skyscraper, butt-dial . . .

Duke (Ellington and Wayne)

Rocky (Marciano, Balboa, Colavito)

Wait!—We'll double your order, but you have to call NOW! Have your credit card ready . . .

 Writing Student: *I feel bad when I talk to someone majoring in Double E or Astro.*
 Writing Teacher: *I know, it's like seeing someone in a wheelchair.*

Botoxed.

Avoid disappointment and future regret—Call NOW!

The can opener, with its two rolling wheels and twist key, was invented five years after my father was born.

Amateurs believe in the possibility of many solutions while experts believe in a few. Some of our best insights come to us by way of unjaded beginners.

Self-Esteem:
Fear of success and fear of failure are the same thing.

. . . and is NOT available in stores!

Are tragedy and banality intertwined?

Why would you hire an interior decorator, with their puffy curtains and wooden geese? I don't want dead branches. Valence? Who the fuck needs a valence?

A trillion dollars is to a million dollars as a million dollars is to one dollar.

Each year, Americans waste an estimated 160 billion pounds of food—enough to fill the Rose Bowl to the brim.

If you order NOW—Free shipping!

Freedom's just another word for nothin' left to lose . . .

Kris Kristofferson is the son of an air force general, who encouraged a military career. Kristofferson boxed Golden Gloves and attended Pomona College, from where he was awarded a Rhodes scholarship to study literature at Oxford. He eventually joined the army, but come 1965, resigned his officer's commission for a career in music. He had just been assigned to teach English at West Point.

Edgar Allen Poe attended West Point for a semester.

Songwriter Harry Chapin attended the Air Force Academy for part of a semester.

The house my father was born in passed down to his Aunt Gayle, my grandmother Anderson's baby sister. The house sat in the center of Lehi, Utah, near the church and school and courthouse and drugstore. When we visited each summer, I would sleep on the porch with Aunt Gayle's sons who were my age. The porch was enclosed by towering, flowering lilacs. When we drove north to Montana, we'd cart along fresh-picked cherries and sprigs of dead lilacs for seeds.

Lilac, gooseberries, forsythia, iris, rhubarb.

The thing about Philippe Petit's high-wire walk between the Twin Towers of the World Trade Center is that it cannot be replicated.

Juba.

If God exists, it doesn't make sense to think of him as the tooth fairy, say.

Mohamed Bouazizi.

An old man with a TV remote control was circling the condo pool. He would stop to click the clicker at you. His daughter, in her sixties, was circling too, apologizing for her father. We made it simple for her by smiling, nodding. What I wanted to say was that her father—the former judge—was on the right track, as he was just trying to change the picture.

But no one can deny that God per se is invisible, or deny that his voice is very still, very small, or explain why.—Annie Dillard

Shibboleth.

Doo-bop-choo-bop.

There are 18 homeless to every owned American car, so you can't donate your car to cover them for shelter.

Graffito:
Don't Believe Everything You Think

War to End All Wars:
In WWI, over half of France's males died, ages 20 to 32.

Florida:
Palm trees and Walgreen's and gobs of white paint.

Dick and Jane and Sally and Spot and Puff.

We understand the world by how we retrieve memories, re-order informa-tion into stories to justify how we feel.—Stephen Elliott

Only a fool mistakes memory for fact.—Ibid.

How to Name Florida Apartments *Not* within Walking Distance or Even Sight of the Atlantic:
Bayview, Ocean Manor, Ocean Club, Shore Arms, Seaside, Sea Watch, Sea Tower, By-the-Sea, Playa del Mar, Ocean Vue, Oceanside, The Galleon, Sun 'n' Sand, Beach Front . . .

When he laid out the Glen Oriole acreage development, when he ironed woodland and dipping meadow into a glenless, orioleless, sunburnt flat prickly with small boards displaying the names of imaginary streets, he righteously put in a complete sewage-system.—Sinclair Lewis

Maidenform.

There are no facts, only interpretations.—Friedrich Nietzsche

Coppertone.

Even though, as a species, we think with *words*, is it possible that a proper definition of a mystical or spiritual experience is that it is *wordless*?

Apparently knowledge affects taste; that is, food psychologists have told people that they were drinking $200 wine when, in fact, they weren't, and they loved it. "You want a kid to eat carrots?" the psychologists ask. "Pull carrots from a McDonald's bag—they will eat carrots."

My father knew about mushrooms—which you could eat and which you could not. After a rain, he would scour the cow field to bring safe mushrooms home. Can you do this?

Emmett Till.

If we had a keen vision and feeling of all ordinary human life, it would be like hearing the grass grow and the squirrel's heart beat, and we should die of that roar which lies on the other side of silence. As it is, the quickest of us walk about well wadded with stupidity.—George Eliot

James Meredith.

How to End an Audacious Novel:
Yossarian jumped. Nately's whore was hiding just outside the door. The knife came down, missing him by inches, and he took off.—Joseph Heller

How to Audaciously Start One:
Howdy, I'm the Holy Ghost. Talk about your omniscient narrators.
—Jack Butler

Speaking of Writers:
Nothing Paul West has written, whatever its length or purpose, can be labeled *slight*.

What I Learned about Language Chancing upon a Wine Critic:
Jennifer Rosen writes about wine, and she took a poet with her to a tasting. Consider which approach to this tasting serves you best. Three examples:

ARIEL BRUT CUVÉE—
Jennifer: Off-dry, tiny bubbles, white flowers and creamy custard.
Peter: You're 15 years old, it's November, you're walking home through an orchard of frozen apples, your feet are wet, and the girl you took to the movies didn't kiss you.

FRÉ BRUT—
Jennifer: Pungent fruit, lively acid, salty, long finish.
Peter: A steel hull bumping against a dock piling in a stiff wind.

INGLENOOK ST. REGIS RESERVE CABERNET—
Jennifer: Dry earth, cedar, licorice and black pepper with a burst of black cherry and a long, spicy finish.
Peter: A thin, dusty, old carnival worker, chewing gum in the sun.
—Jennifer Rosen

Entr'acte

While missionarying in Belgium and France, I transferred by rail from Bruxelles to Belfort, near the Alsace border. Enroute, I stopped to aid an American who was purchasing sundries in a railroad depot. I'd lived in Bruxelles six months and my French was faulty but better than this fellow citizen's, who thanked me, then slipped off with his stuff. Arrived in Belfort, I straddled my bicycle to the address of my companion missionary's apartment, seeking directions along the way, and stopping to buy hard rolls and bottled milk. Unknown to me, I'd been followed by the French police, who waited outside the apartment some 30 minutes before bursting in, at which time they stacked me in a corner, ransacked my luggage, overturned my bed's mattress, and searched the closet where I'd hung my coat. Then cuffing me, they pushed me into the back of their van-like truck. *Le Préfet* was fortyish, short-haired and tanned, muscled. He questioned me about my train trip. I did my best with my French to explain it. I kept asking what *was* the problem—*Le probleme? Le probleme?*—and where *was* the U.S. Embassy—*Je suis American! Je suis American! Le Préfet* theatrically pocketed my passport, which he'd had me set on his desk. He had one of his assistants then remove my belt, shoelaces, and tie. When I queried this, he replied in slow French, with gestures, that he would not have me hang myself. Why would I?—*Mais pourquoi?* I asked. *Le Préfet* hoisted a newspaper announcing in bold print (as best as I could make it out) that an American GI had shot a gendarme, a French motorcycle cop, who had died. I said, "Who—not me!" I kept pointing at the newspaper, then at myself, over and over, shaking my head. *Non moi! Non moi!* The two cops who had brought me to the station took me by the arms down several flights of stairs, past the ground floor, past the basement into what were surely medieval depths where I would encounter rats and bones and spores of Black Plague. I was installed in an unlighted room with a metal door that slammed with a clang and ramming bolts. In time, the blade of light knifing beneath the windowless door illumined the room just enough for me to make out a concrete block that was to serve as a bed, a waist-high basin and tap, and a corner hole-in-the-floor for a toilet. The place smelled of all that you imagine. It dawned on me that no one knew where I was. Not my parents, not my country, not my church, not even my missionary companion who had been absent from the

apartment when I'd arrived. No one had read me my rights. They didn't do that in France? Hadn't the French helped us in the Revolution? I felt cold. I felt hungry. I pictured my hard rolls and milk. I ran the water in the basin, but it had an odor and I didn't drink. I knew I was alone and that's how I felt. I passed the night, kneeling now and again, at the base of the door, to read my watch, which was the single item the police had left me. What I didn't know was that *Le Préfet*, on checking my status, had confirmed I was American, and was, as I'd claimed, a missionary, and that I'd merely helped an American who spoke less French than I. As I was to find out, that American was the guilty AWOL soldier, and that, at the very least, I'd been suspected of transporting the murder weapon the police never found. Sometime the next morning, I was returned to the headquarters office, some five stories from where I'd been held. *Le Préfet* handed everything back and seemed embarrassed. The thought of counter damage had not occurred. In fact, as I was threading my belt and lacing my shoes I was deciding how best to express my thanks. I blurted: *Vous êtes jolie!* What I'd meant to say was, *Vous êtes gentil!*—*jolie* signifying *pretty*, *gentil* signifying *kind*. *Le Préfet* then announced in perfect English: "I knew you Mormons were polygamists, but don't start telling me I'm pretty!" He laughed, and for the time I worked in Belfort we were cordial friends, and he and his pretty Algerian wife often fed us. His English was such that he knew the names of dry flies: *woolly bugger, royal coachman, elk-hair caddis*. His vocabulary included words like *ginger snap* and *Bronx* and *hackle*. He'd been a double agent in Morocco during the war, who had worked with the Brits. His affection for things American had to do with the effort and manner with which the Allies had won the war. He owned records by Roy Acuff, Ernest Tubbs, Hank Snow.

The snow came down last night like moths
Burned on the moon; it fell till dawn,
Covered the town with simple cloths.
—Richard Wilbur, from "First Snow in Alsace"

We read to know we are not alone.—C. S. Lewis

Mehmet Ali Agca.

Of the total energy produced on Earth since the Industrial Revolution began, half has been consumed in just the last twenty years. . . . Today it takes the average citizen of Tanzania almost a year to produce the same volume of carbon emissions as is effortlessly generated every two and a half days by a European, or every twenty-eight hours by an American.
—Bill Bryson

Eadweard Muybridge.

In Britain, the founding of the Society for the Prevention of Cruelty to Animals occurred 60 years before such a society for children.

It is remarkable to think that we had had electric lights and telephones for about as long as we have known that germs kill people.—Bill Bryson

[Alexander] Bell lived to complete the first call from New York to San Francisco, which required 14,000 miles of copper wire and 130,000 telephone poles.—Eula Biss

Graffito:
Guns Kill People Like Spoons Make Fat People Eat

Zsa Zsa Gabor was still a bombshell when I grew old enough to notice. Today's paper reported that her right leg above the knee has been amputated to contain an infection stemming from her hip replacement last summer. Zsa Zsa is 93.

Plop, plop, fizz, fizz. Oh, what a relief it is.

Alka-Seltzer is basically aspirin and baking soda.

My grandfather after drinking, drank eggs, raw eggs.

What the Scientists Say:
The light from the farthest known galaxy has taken 13.2 billion years to

reach us. Given the speed of light, how to comprehend such distance? For one who grasps this distance should come the obligation to explain what it means.

Within three months of my father's burial, my mother telephoned to say she was remarrying. I congratulated her, then recradling the phone, announced: "That slut!" I was 48 years old, into a second marriage myself, and yet this was my compulsive reaction. I should have known better, but didn't. It's how I felt. In fact, what impressed itself was that, for the first time, I accredited Hamlet.

Is what interests us in the mirror not ourselves but that the person we see looks so interested in us?

That it should come to this,
But two months dead, nay not so much, not two
So excellent a king . . . frailty, thy name is woman.
—Shakespeare, *Hamlet*, I, ii

Bottom line: Olympic gold
can't buy a black man
a Louisville hamburger
in nineteen-sixty.
—Elizabeth Alexander, from "Narrative: Ali"

Real Estate Tip:
Buy the smallest house in the best neighborhood.

Fewer people died at Pearl Harbor than at Ground Zero.

There's an algae that secretes oil (of the bio-fuel type) and consumes CO_2?

She had a Mount Rushmore T-shirt on, and those guys never looked so good. Especially Jefferson and Lincoln. Kind of bloated but happy.
—Guy Noir

A ream is a lot of paper, sold and purchased blank. Written on, it's a book.
—Sue Allison

Those things about which we cannot theorize, we must narrate.
—Umberto Eco

I met a traveller from an antique land
Who said: "Two vast and trunkless legs of stone
Stand in the desert. Near them on the sand,
Half sunk, a shattered visage lies, whose frown
And wrinkled lip and sneer of cold command
Tell that its sculptor well those passions read
Which yet survive, stamped on these lifeless things,
The hand that mocked them and the heart that fed.
And on the pedestal these words appear:
"My name is Ozymandias, King of Kings:
Look on my works, ye mighty, and despair!"
Nothing beside remains. Round the decay
Of that colossal wreck, boundless and bare,
The lone and level sands stretch far away.
—Percy Bysshe Shelley, "Ozymandias"

Is memory what happened or how you felt about what happened?

Wanna live forever? Be a metaphor.—Myra Sklarew

It was the green-walled cafeteria of my high school in which I and my classmates were informed that President Kennedy had been shot. Before lunch was over, he had died. Did we return to class?

The dawn rises like sick old men playing on the rooftops in their underwear.
—Stuart Dybek

Vaughn Meader was such a successful professional impersonator of the president that Kennedy once greeted a group from the Democratic National Committee by saying, "Vaughn Meader was busy tonight so I

came myself." After Kennedy died, Meader's much-sought-after schtick lost all appeal and he spiraled into oblivion and heroin.

Tina Fey.

So: Raymond Carver knew about hooch and could write about it, too. In one poem he presents a man who downs Listerine by the case, like a vagrant Russian might seek radiator coolant. Then finishing the poem with what could be autobiographical insight: *Fixed / myself a nice glass of NyQuil. / Dragged a chair over to the window. / Where I watched a pale moon struggle to rise / over Cupertino, California . . .*

The nighttime, sniffling, sneezing, coughing, aching, fever, best sleep you ever got with a cold . . . medicine.

It makes no difference what men think of war, said the judge. War endures. As well ask men what they think of stone. War was always here. Before man was, war waited for him. The ultimate trade awaiting its ultimate practitioner. That is the way it was and will be. . . . War is god.
—Cormac McCarthy

What is walking but controlled falling?

William Devane jumpstarted his acting career by portraying John Kennedy in a TV movie about the Cuban Missile Crisis. *The Missiles of October* screened in 1974. Eight years earlier—three years after John had died and two years before Robert would—Devane portrayed Robert in an off-Broadway spoof. Devane's father had been FDR's chauffeur when Roosevelt was the governor of New York.

How to Write about Kids:
*North Country children
teach you how to know
the black from the grizzly:
Climb a tree. The black
will come up to get you:*

197

the grizzly, who can't
climb, will shake you down
"like a plum." It is
an argument they make
against going to school.
—Robley Wilson Jr., "Bears"

Georg Philipp Telemann was, at the time, more famous than his fellow composer, Bach. He and Johann were friends; in fact, Telemann was godfather to Bach's son, Carl Philipp Emanuel Bach.

Dick Cheney contemplating a heart transplant?

"Colder than a witch's tit," my wife will say when the temperature drops. Although uncertain as to how cold this would be, it does seem as if it would be so, right?

Jihad Jane.

Along with chimpanzees, orangutans, and gorillas, bonobos are great apes. Bonobos, though, share more than 98 percent of the same genetic make-up as humans. Bonobo society is peaceful, matriarchal, and egalitarian. These sweet creatures live in large groups where harmonious coexistence is the norm. They are not known to solve problems by fighting. Scientists remain perplexed.

How to Conclude a Movie:
Alvy and Annie shake hands and kiss each other friendly like. Annie crosses the street, Alvy watching her go. Then he turns, and slowly walks down the street offscreen. His voice is heard over the scene:
ALVY'S VOICE-OVER *After that it got pretty late. And we both hadda go, but it was great seeing Annie again, right? I realized what a terrific person she was and—and how much fun it was just knowing her and I—I thought of that old joke, you know, this—this—this guy goes to a psychiatrist and says, "Doc, uh, my brother's crazy. He thinks he's a chicken." And, uh, the doctor says, "Well, why don't you turn him in?" and the guy says, "I would, but I need the eggs." Well, I guess that's pretty much how*

I feel about relationships. You know, they're totally irrational and crazy and absurd and . . . but, uh, I guess we keep goin' through it because, uh, most of us need the eggs. —Woody Allen

Bonobos often copulate face-to-face, looking into one another's eyes, like people.

Joaquín Rodrigo.

Boxing in the Movies:
You was my brother, Charley, you shoulda looked out for me a little bit.
—Terry Malloy, *On the Waterfront*

Cut me, Mick. —Rocky Balboa, *Rocky*

I got these small hands. I got a little girl's hands.
—Jake La Motta, *Raging Bull*

I admit to have long admired boxing (and boxers), though it does now, at 65, occur to me that the sport, like war, concerns itself with fear, pain, damage, loss, disbelief, defiance, shame, blood, humiliation, resentment, blame, courage, sorrow . . .

Let me have a war, say I: It exceeds peace as far as day
Does night; it's spritely, waking, audible, full of vent.
Peace is a very apoplexy, lethargy, mull'd, deaf, sleepy,
Insensible; a getter of more bastard children than war is a
Destroyer of men.
—Shakespeare, *Coriolanus*, IV, v

Yo, Adrian!

The myth of war entices us with the allure of heroism. But the images of war handed to us, even when they are graphic, leave out the one essential element of war—fear. There is until the actual moment of confrontation, no cost to imagining glory. The visual and audio effects of films, the battlefield descriptions in books, make the experience appear real. In fact the

experience is sterile. We are safe. We do not smell rotting flesh, hear the cries of agony, or see before us blood and entrails seeping out of bodies. We view, from a distance, the rush, the excitement, but feel none of the awful gut-wrenching anxiety and humiliation that come with mortal danger. It takes the experience of fear and the chaos of battle, the deafening and disturbing noise, to wake us up, to make us realize that we are not who we imagined we were, that war as displayed by the entertainment industry might, in most cases, as well be ballet. But even with this I have seen soldiers in war try to recreate the fiction of war, especially when a television camera is around to record the attempted heroics. The result is usually pathetic.—Chris Hedges

We go forward to defend freedom and all that is good and just in the world . . .—George W. Bush

Were only patriotism as simple as a bigger flag . . .

Have your credit card ready . . .

One of my daughters, each ski season for a number of years, would lose her left glove, making it impossible to mix and match. Between the ages, say, of 6 and 13, I bought a new pair each season. Do you know a child with only one hand, a right hand?

Two Ski Rules:
(1) Never ski down a run without stopping.
(2) Always stop in the sun.

Attention equals life or is its only evidence.—Frank O'Hara

How to Title a Memoir:
I'm Sorry You Feel That Way: The Astonishing but True Story of a Daughter, Sister, Slut, Wife, Mother, and Friend to Man and Dog—Diana Joseph

When Fulton J. Sheen was asked what it was like to hear nuns' confessions, he said, "Like being stoned with popcorn."

Remember Sheen—who understood TV early on—a Catholic priest joking and preening for an electronic audience, eyeballing the crowd? Though we only ever had a black-and-white while I lived at home, I could tell that part of the bishop's suit was colored: red, light purple, rose?

A priest friend of my uncle Earl used to take me and Uncle Earl's son (also named Earl) on daytrips to West Yellowstone. We would lunch on trout and compare the geysers before driving home.

. . . no amount of literary palaver will appease boxing's critics or transform the sport into a vocation like any other. It's not. It's a brutal business, and if a valid defense exists we must look to the boxers themselves, not because disenfranchised young men benefit from boxing (few actually do) but because once in the professional ranks they deal in a level of violence incomprehensible to outsiders. The violence they mete out is not only harder than most civilians can fathom; it is also accommodated in certain unfathomable ways. A fighter is his body, and it is as a body that he expresses himself. At the same time, he is also curiously detached from it: a body is something to be used like a tool or worn like armor. In short, his sense of himself as something designed to deliver and accept punishment is what enables him to do—and protects him from—violence.

But however routine such violence becomes to the professional, a fight is still a nasty bit of work. It is not, as some writers like to claim, an aesthetic enactment, erotic dance, savage ceremony, or chess match; it's not even a dialogue except in the limited sense than an exchange occurs between two individuals. A fight is a fight, although in the more interesting ones a man's skill, courage, and grace can make us briefly forget the end to which they are being put.—Arthur Krystal

If we could save one Brit and one American, it would be Shakespeare and Melville, right?

These fragments I have shored against my ruin . . .

The problem with emperors who wear no clothes is not that they have no clothes but that they choose to trust they have a fine tailor.

. . . Somewhere around eleven thousand years ago, some clever hunting human primates—who made stone spears, drew pictures, and talked—had another idea. They knocked ripe seeds from transplanted wild barley or einkorn wheat and stored the seeds dry at their campsite in the Zagros Mountains. Since eating ground seed kept the families alive when hunting failed, they settled there, planted more seed, hunkered down to wait its sprouting, and, what with one thing and another, shucks, here we be. I at my laptop computer, you with a book in your hands. We are just like squirrels, really, or, well, more like gibbons, but we happen to use tools, speak, and write; we blundered into art and science. We are one of those animals, the ones whose neocortexes swelled, who just happen to write en-cyclopedias and fly to the moon. Can anyone believe this?—Annie Dillard

Solar Farm.

The private terror of the liberal spirit is invariably suicide, not murder.
—Norman Mailer

Tiananmen.

You called for night; it falls: now cry in darkness.—Samuel Beckett

Remix.

One Notion of Hell:
You're duct-taped to a tree, forced to listen to Debbie Boone sing "You Light Up My Life" forever.

When you purchase your third clothes dryer, you've probably purchased your last. Think about it.

How can we enjoy memoirs, believing them to be true, when nothing, as everyone knows, is so unreliable as memory? Many memoirs make a virtue of seeming unadorned, unvarnished, but the first and most un-forgettable thing we learn about memory is that it's fallible. Memories, we now know, can be buried, lost, blocked, repressed, even recovered. We remember what suits us, and there's almost no limit to what we can

forget. Only those who keep faithful diaries will know what they were doing at this time, on this day, a year ago. The rest of us recall only the most intense moments, and even these tend to have been mythologized by repetition into well-wrought chapters in the story of our lives. To this extent, memoirs really can claim to be modern novels, all the way down to the presence of an unreliable narrator.—David Shields

How to Conclude an Essay:
You can brick up your heart as stout and tight and hard and cold and impregnable as you possibly can and down it comes in an instant, felled by a woman's second glance, a child's apple breath, the shatter of glass in the road, the words "I have something to tell you," a cat with a broken spine dragging itself into the forest to die, the brush of your mother's papery ancient hand in the thicket of your hair, the memory of your father's voice in the morning echoing from the kitchen where he is making pancakes for his children.—Brian Doyle

In Pittsburg, Kansas, a black man was hanged from a telephone pole, cut down, burned, shot, and stoned with bricks. "At first the negro was defiant," the New York Times *reported, "but just before he was hanged he begged hard for his life."*—Eula Biss

Graffito:
Hide from your TV

The past is a foreign country: they do things differently there.
—L. P. Hartley

Night soil.

Srebrenica.

Darwin Award:
At the radar site in Alaska, I stopped an airman trying to hand-feed a 400-pound black bear Doritos in an attempt to capture a Kodak moment for his fiancée back in Missouri, the "Show-Me" state. He'd poured a trail of honey to him and his bag of chips.

Two of the women were in their twenties, the third was an old lady. Someone had shot her in the mouth and her shattered dentures cascaded with her own teeth down her front like mashed melon pips. One girl had been shot repeatedly in the chest. It was difficult to tell whether the other had had her throat cut or been shot; a great gash of blood crescented her neck. The expression on their faces had survived the damage. It was so clear. A time-valve that opened directly on to those last moments. So you saw what they saw. I hope beyond hope that I never see it again.

In the recess of the shed something moved. It was a cow. The only survivor in Stupni Do. Someone had pulled a large plastic barrel over its head. The neck of the barrel fitted tightly around that of the beast, whose horns impaled the sides, keeping it locked in place. It must have taken a great amount of time and energy to bring the cow to this state: unable to see or eat.

So that was how we spent our last few minutes in the dusk in Stupni Do. Fighting the impulse that wanted our legs to kick us out of that place as fast and far away as possible, wrestling in a shed with a cow and a plastic barrel watched by three murdered women. Pulling and cursing and grunting with a torch that barely worked and a pathetic penknife because we wanted the cow to live. We wanted the cow to be able to see and eat again. We wanted that more than anything.—Anthony Loyd

Peace seems to allow so little space for belief in destiny, fate, God, or ghosts. —Ibid.

In a war without aim, you tend not to aim. You close your eyes, close your heart. The consequences become hit or miss in the most literal sense. —Tim O'Brien, from "The Vietnam in Me"

Reading is creative listening that alters the reader. Books are remembered consciously in pictures and words, but they are also present in the strange, shifting rooms of our unconsciousness. Others, which for some reason have no power to rearrange our lives, are often forgotten entirely. The ones that stay with us, however, become us, part of the mysterious workings of the human mind that translates little symbols on a page into real experience.—Siri Hustvedt

Supplemental Advice:
Do not immerse in water.
Zip your coat.
Trust haiku.
Don't eat yellow snow.
Walk with scissors.
Always bet on black.
Pas Fumer.
Don't buy surplus ammo from India.
Let your children paint their bedrooms.
Pack Tabasco for long trips to remote locations.
Good chili requires cumin.
Watch your step.
Pay attention.
If nine Russians tell you you're drunk—lie down.
Keep in mind that the nearest exit may be behind you.
Use less stuff.
Can the head. Bomb the gut.
Floss.

Dugway Proving Ground is a U.S. Army facility located in southern Tooele County in Utah. Encompassing over 800,000 acres of the Great Salt Lake Desert, it is an area the size of the state of Rhode Island, surrounded on three sides by mountain ranges. After Pearl Harbor, the Department of Defense pushed for expanded capability and knowledge of chemical and biological warfare. Dugway was established to test weapons and defenses.

Graffito:
Remember When Sex Was Dirty And The Air Was Clean?

The term "dugway" comes from a pioneer technique to dig a trench along a hillside to keep a wagon from tipping.

In 1968, American troops reach their highest levels in Vietnam, and more Americans die that year than during any other single year of the war. In March of that year, 6,000 sheep die in Skull Valley, 30 miles

from Dugway's ample testing grounds. The Dugway sheep incident coincided with several open-air tests of the nerve agent VX. The army admits no liability, but does pay the ranchers for their losses. The air-dispersal missions may have been conducted by the air force out of Hill Air Force Base, near Ogden, Utah.

Among materials and methods tested at Dugway: toxic agents, flame-throwers, chemical spray systems, biological warfare weapons, fire-bombing tactics, antidotes for chemical agents, protective clothing . . .

January 2011. A vial containing 1 ml (a quarter of a teaspoon) of nerve agent VX was mislabeled and erroneously stored, causing a 12-hour lockdown of Dugway Proving Ground until the vial was found. "All personnel are uninjured and safe," the facility said in a news release. "The public is safe as well."

Armaments, universal debt, and planned obsolescence—those are the three pillars of Western prosperity.—Aldous Huxley

VX is an amber-colored, odorless, and tasteless oily liquid that does not evaporate easily unless temperatures are high, officials say. "It evapo-rates slowly, like motor oil."

Victims are exposed to the agent through skin contact, eye contact, or inhalation. VX affects the body's ability to carry messages through the nerves. It kills sheep.

Coda:
In July 1970, in Tooele, Utah, I killed a pig with a fire hose. I'd gradu-ated Utah State, with a bachelor's degree in English. My first wife and I and daughter had moved to Tooele to be nearer Salt Lake City and the University of Utah, where I'd enrolled in an English MA program in order to remain in ROTC in order to be commissioned into the air force. I was broke, didn't own a car. We had spent what tuition money we had for the birth of our daughter. My parents came to the rescue, said we could live with them for the year it would take to attend gradu-ate school, to get the commission and a paying job in the air force. One

July Saturday afternoon, everyone was gone, my daughter asleep in the house. My father was in his office at the smelter catching up on safety reports. He had been sent down from Butte by the Anaconda Company to straighten out the poor safety record at the smelter that was producing lead, the majority of which, no doubt, was making its way to Southeast Asia. During the week, I worked the swing shift at the smelter. I'd shower-up at midnight, then make my way to the garage where my father had set up lighting and a table where I could do my work. I'd study for a couple of hours, then go to bed to wake by 6 to make my morning classes at the U of U. It was a 40-mile drive to Salt Lake, along the salt flats, a roundtrip I made each day in my father's old GMC truck, each roundtrip requiring a quart of oil. He'd bought the algae-colored pickup at an auction at the Tooele Army Depot. Attending morning classes at the university, I'd do my library work before returning to Tooele for my afternoon shift at the smelter. It was dirty work and hot. Worker injuries were mostly burns and smashed appendages.

An ingot mold is a place to pour leftover molten metal after casting, a practice called *pigging out* in the foundry craft, with the resulting ingots called *pigs*. A worker too lazy to walk around a field of molds was hopping from casting to casting when he slipped into one near the edge. Molten lead covered and filled his right-foot's boot. A fellow worker hit the boot with a stream of water, in an attempt to cool the lead, but what he managed was to congeal the bootlaces so the boot could not be removed before he had steam-cooked the man's foot inside. It was a weekend shift, about 10 at night, and we heard the man's screams from our house. Following futile attempts at healing, the man's foot was removed, and he was rehired as a permanent night watchman. Now and again, that year I worked at the smelter, I subbed for him. I liked the job in that I could study and still make the appointed rounds to the smelter's tinder outposts and abandoned furnaces that the company was certain some disgruntled worker would want to burn down.

The safety engineer's house was located adjacent to the smelter to ensure quick response around the clock, all three of the eight-hour shifts. My father needed permission (and to have in his possession a radio walkie-talkie) in order to depart the premises. His radius of absence was 25 miles. On the day in question, as I say, everyone but my daughter and I was gone, and she was asleep in the house. I'd been

reading Edmund Spenser and left the house for a break. The pig in its pen looked hot. Next to the pen was an honest-to-god rolled-up fire hose—not the garden-variety sort! A hundred feet of large-diameter, heavy canvas hosing! The fire hose had been installed in the event of a house fire caused by airborne cinders from the plant's two working furnaces. So: I was a college graduate, a husband and father—an almost air force officer—and I should have known better, but I unrolled the hose and fired it up. The hose was difficult to control, but I managed to aim it, finally, straight at the pig. I hit him dead on and bowled him over. He seemed to expire at once. Years after, someone explained that pigs can't sweat and therefore can't handle sudden temperature shifts. How do you look up something like that—do you know? By the time I got the hose shut off, the pig was dead and the pen afloat with mud. It was a scene of disaster, as if a Thai village had been hit by killer monsoons. For a fleeting moment, I had the thought of a kid: *Maybe no one will notice.* But I knew someone would, so I started what seemed now the long walk to my father's office. I felt about 14. I have to say my father was pretty good about it. We walked home together, strung up the pig, and cut its throat. Because the pig had been dead for a while, my father, after opening the throat, found the heart and hand-pumped it in an effort to expel pooled blood. Can you see him, fist in the pig, compressing? Do you see him?

Works Cited

Abbott, Lee K. *All Things, All at Once*. New York: Norton, 2006.

"Abu Ghraib Convictions." Fast Facts. <http://www.foxnews.com/story/ 0,2933,170603,00.html>

Ackerman, Diane. *The Zookeeper's Wife*. New York: Norton, 2007.

Alexander, Elizabeth. "Narrative: Ali." In *Perfect in Their Art: Poems on Boxing from Homer to Ali*, edited by Robert Hedin and Michael Waters. Carbondale: Southern Illinois University Press, 2003.

Alexander the Great. <www.brainyquote.com>

Ali, Muhammad. <www.brainyquote.com>

Allen, Woody. *Four Films of Woody Allen*. London: Faber, 1983.

Allison, Sue. "Taking a Reading." In *The Best American Essays*, edited by Mary Oliver. New York: Mariner, 2009.

Anderson, Donald, ed. *Aftermath: An Anthology of Post-Vietnam Fiction*. New York: Henry Holt, 1995.

———. "AWOL." *North American Review*, 296.2: 36.

———. *Fire Road*. Iowa City: University of Iowa Press, 2001.

———. "Legal Limit." *Michigan Quarterly Review*, XLII.3: 546–47.

———. "Plus ça change . . ." *North American Review*, 290.5: 56.

———. "Rock Salt." EPOCH, 56.2: 189–203.

———. "Sao Paulo," unpublished.

———. "Scaling Ice." *SUB-Terrain*, 2.17: 20–21.

———. "Soldier-Artists: Preserving the World." *Connecticut Review*, 32.2: 23–35.

———. "Some People Who May Appear In My Next Story." *North American Review*, 294.2: 34–35.

———. "Stumps." *North American Review*, 289.1: 3.

———. "Stunted." *North American Review*, 290.3&4: 76–77.

———. "Tell Me A Story." In *Writers on Writing*, edited by Maurice Lee. Westport, CT: Praeger, 2005.

———, ed. *When War Becomes Personal: Soldiers' Accounts from the Civil War to Iraq*. Iowa City: University of Iowa Press, 2008.

Appleman, Philip. *Open Doorways*. New York: Norton, 1976.

Arendt, Hannah. *Eichmann in Jerusalem: A Report on the Banality of Evil*. New York: Penguin, 2006.

Armagost, Jason. "These Four Archaic Truths and Martial Virtues." *Connecticut Review*, 32.2: 81.

Atwood, Margaret. *Selected Poems, 1965–1975, Volume 1.* Boston: Houghton Mifflin, 1976.

Balaban, John. *Path, Crooked Path.* Port Townsend, WA: Copper Canyon, 2006.

Baldwin, James. *Notes of a Native Son.* Boston: Beacon Press, 1984.

Banks, Russell. *Hamilton Stark.* Boston: Houghton Mifflin, 1978.

Barthes, Roland. *A Lover's Discourse: Fragments.* New York: Hill and Wang, 2010.

Becker, Elizabeth. *When the War Was Over: Cambodia and the Khmer Rouge Revolution.* New York: PublicAffairs, 1998.

Beckett, Samuel. *Endgame.* London: Faber, 1976.

———. *Waiting for Godot.* New York: Grove, 1977.

Bellow, Saul. *Letters.* Edited by Benjamin Taylor. New York: Viking, 2010.

Bishop, Jonathan. *Emerson on the Soul.* New York: AMS Press, 1993.

Biss, Eula. *Notes from No Man's Land: American Essays.* Minneapolis: Graywolf Press, 2009.

Bourjaily, Vance. *Confessions of a Spent Youth.* New York: William Morrow, 1986.

Bowen, Catherine Drinker. In *Creativity and the Writing Process,* edited by Olivia Bertagnolli and Jeff Rackman. New York: John Wiley & Sons, 1982.

Bowen, Kevin, and Bruce Weigl, eds. *Writing between the Lines.* Amherst: University of Massachusetts Press, 1997.

Boyle, T. C. <http://www.denverpost.com/books/ci_15832072>

Bredahl, A. Carl, Jr. *New Ground: Western American Narrative and the Literary Canon.* Chapel Hill: University of North Carolina Press, 2009.

Bryson, Bill. *At Home: A Short History of Private Life.* New York: Doubleday, 2010.

Busch, Frederick. *Hard Water Country: Stories.* New York: Knopf, 1979.

Butler, Jack. *Living in Little Rock with Miss Little Rock.* New York: Knopf, 1993.

Caligula. <www.imdb.com/title/tt0080491/quotes>

Camus, Albert. *Notebooks 1951–1959.* Lanham, MD: Ivan R. Dee, 2008.

Carver, Raymond. *All of Us: The Collected Poems.* New York: Vintage, 2000.

Cheever, John. *The Wapshot Chronicle.* New York: Harper Perennial Modern Classics, 2011.

Child, Lee. *Gone Tomorrow.* New York: Delacorte, 2009.

Cocteau, Jean. In *Marcel Proust: A Life,* by William C. Carter. New Haven: Yale University Press, 2002.

Collins, Billy. <http://www.poetryfoundation.org/poem/176056>

Connell, Evan S. *Deus Lo Volt!: A Chronicle of the Crusades.* New York: Counterpoint, 2001.

Considine, Glenn D. *Van Nostrand's Scientific Encyclopedia.* Hoboken NJ: John Wiley & Sons, 2002.

Copper Camp: Stories of the World's Greatest Mining Town, Butte, Montana. Edited by Writers' Project of Montana. New York: Hastings House, 1943.

Crane, Stephen. *The Black Riders and Other Lines.* Forgotten Books, 2010.

Cummings, E. E. *100 Selected Poems.* New York: Grove Press, 1994.

Darwin, Charles. *The Works of Charles Darwin, Volume 16: The Origin of Species, 1876*. New York: New York University Press, 2010.

Derbyshire, John. <http://www.johnderbyshire.com/Opinions/Straggler/033. html>

Dickens, Charles. *A Tale of Two Cities*. New York: Penguin Classics, 2011.

Dillard, Annie. *For the Time Being*. New York: Vintage, 2000.

Distelheim, Rochelle. "The Kiss-Me-Quick." *North American Review*, 275.3: 42.

Doyle, Brian. *The Wet Engine: Exploring the Mad Wild Miracle of Heart*. Orleans, MA: Paraclete Press, 2005.

Dubac, Robert. <www.robertdubac.com/freerangethinking.html>

Dubus, Andre. *Broken Vessels*. Boston: Godine, 1992.

Dunnigan, James F. *How to Make War: A Comprehensive Guide to Modern Warfare in the 21st Century*. New York: Harper, 1982.

Dybek, Stuart. "Blight." In *The Coast of Chicago: Stories*. New York: Picador, 2004.

Eco, Umberto. <www.creativewritingquotes.com>

Ehrhart, W. D. *Busted: A Vietnam Veteran in Nixon's America*. Amherst: University of Massachusetts Press, 1995.

Eisenhower, Dwight David. <www.harpers.org/archive/2007/11/hbc-90001660>

Eliot, George. *Middlemarch*. New York: Simon & Brown, 2011.

Elliott, Stephen. *The Adderall Diaries*. Minneapolis: Graywolf Press, 2010.

Filkins, Dexter. *The Forever War*. New York: Vintage, 2008.

Flaubert, Gustave. *Madame Bovary*. New York: Penguin Classics, 2002.

Foch, Ferdinand. <www.brainyquote.com>

Foreman, George. <http://espn.go.com/classic/biography/s/Frazier_Joe.html>

France, Anatole. In *The Portable Curmudgeon*, edited by Jon Winokur. New York: Plume, 1992.

Francis, Robert. *Collected Poems 1936–1976*. Amherst: University of Massachusetts Press, 1985.

Frankel, Max. "McNamara's Retreat." In *New York Times*, April 16, 1995.

Frederick the Great. <www.great-quotes.com>

Freud, Sigmund. *Collected Papers: Character and Culture*. New York: Collier Books, 1963.

Fussell, Paul. *Thank God for the Atom Bomb*. New York: Ballantine, 1990.

Galeano, Eduardo. *Memory of Fire III: Century of the Wind*. New York: Pantheon, 1988.

Gass, William. *On Being Blue: A Philosophical Inquiry*. Boston: Godine, 1976.

Gellhorn, Martha. *Reporting Vietnam: Part One*. New York: Library of America, 1998.

Gourevitch, Philip. *We Wish to Inform You That Tomorrow We Will Be Killed with Our Families: Stories from Rwanda*. New York: Picador, 1998.

Greene, Graham. *The Quiet American*. New York: Penguin, 1996.

Grizzard, Lewis. <www.quotationsbook.com>

Gustafson, Lowell S. *The Sovereignty Dispute over the Falkland (Malvinas) Islands*. New York: Oxford University Press, 1988.

Guston, Philip. <www.aestheticrealism.org/Philip_Guston/Philip_Guston.html>

Hass, Robert, ed. *HAIKU: Versions of Bashō, Buson, and Issa*. New York: Ecco, 1994.

Halberstam, David. <http://espn.go.com/classic/biography/s/Frazier_Joe.html>

Hall, Jim. <http://jameswhall.blogspot.com/2008/01/maybe-dats-your-pwoblem-too.html>

Hampl, Patricia. *I Could Tell You Stories: Sojourns in the Land of Memory*. New York: W. W. Norton, 2000.

Handey, Jack. *Deep Thoughts*. New York: Berkley, 1992. Also see <http://www.deepthoughtsbyjackhandey.com>

Hanson, Victor Davis. *Ripples of Battle: How Wars of the Past Still Determine How We Fight, How We Live, and How We Think*. New York: Doubleday, 2003.

Hartley, L. P. *The Go-Between*. New York: NYRB Classics, 2002.

Hedges, Chris. *War Is a Force That Gives Us Meaning*. New York: PublicAffairs, 2002.

Heinlein, Robert. <www.quotationspage.com>

Heller, Joseph. *Catch-22: 50th Anniversary Edition*. New York: Simon & Schuster, 2011.

Hemingway, Ernest. *A Farewell to Arms*. New York: Simon & Schuster, 1995.

———. *In Our Time*. New York: Scribner's, 1970.

Henderson, William. <http://www.the-great-war-society.org/subtheme.html>

Herodotus. <www.thinkexist.com>

Herzog, Tobey C. *Writing War, Writing Life: Caputo, Heinemann, O'Brien, Butler*. Iowa City: University of Iowa Press, 2008.

Hirshfield, Jane. <www.poetrylondon.co.uk>

Hoagland, Edward. *Sex and the River Styx*. White River Junction, VT: Chelsea Green, 2011.

Hoffmann, Yoel, ed. *Japanese Death Poems*. Rutland, VT: Charles E. Tuttle, 1986.

Holiday, Billie. <http://womenshistory.about.com>

Houdini, Harry. <www.thegreatharryhoudini.com>

Hugo, Richard, qtd. in *Creativity and the Writing Process*. Edited by Olivia Bertagnolli and Jeff Rackman. New York: John Wiley & Sons, 1982.

Hustvedt, Siri. "Memory and Ms. Hyde." *Poets & Writers*, May/June 2011: 34–42.

Huxley, Aldous. <www.goodreads.com/author/quotes>

Hynes, Samuel. *The Soldier's Tale: Bearing Witness to Modern War*. New York: Penguin, 1997.

Irwin, Mark. "Poetry & Memorability." *The Writer's Chronicle*, 43.3: 28–32.

Jarman, Mark. <http://rattle.com/blog/2008/11/northern-lights-by-mark-jarman/>

Johnson, Jim. "The Things a Man Keeps." In *The Best of the Prose Poem: An International Journal*, edited by Peter Johnson. Buffalo: White Pine Press, 2000.

Jones, Thom. *The Pugilist at Rest*. New York: Little, Brown, 1993.

Joyce, James. *Dubliners*. New York: Norton Critical Edition, 2006.

Kaus, Mickey. "Who's Sorry Now." *New Republic*, May 1, 1995: 6.

Keats, John. <www.john-keats.com/briefe/221117.htm>

Keller, Helen. *The Story of My Life: The Restored Classic*. New York: Norton, 2004.

Keplinger, David. *The Prayers of Others*. Kalamazoo: New Issues Poetry & Prose, 2006.

Komunyakaa, Yusef. *Dien Cai Dau*. Hanover, NH: Wesleyan University Press, 1988.

Kristof, Nicholas D. <www.nytimes.com/2010/07/29/opinion/29kristof.html>

Krystal, Arthur. *The Half-Life of an American Essayist*. Boston: Godine, 2007.

Kundera, Milan. *The Curtain: An Essay in Seven Parts*. New York: HarperCollins, 2007.

Langewiesche, William. *American Ground: Unbuilding the World Trade Center*. New York: North Point, 2002.

Lapham, Lewis H. "Seen but Not Heard." *Harper's*, July 1995: 29–36.

Lebowitz, Fran. *Social Studies*. New York: Random House, 1981.

LeMay, Curtis E. *Mission with LeMay: My Story*. With MacKinlay Kantor. New York: Doubleday, 1965.

Leonardo da Vinci. <www.brainyquote.com>

Lepore, Jill. *The Name of War: King Philip's War and the Origins of American Identity*. New York: Knopf, 1998.

Levant, Oscar. <www.brainyquote.com>

Lewis, C. S. <www.thinkexist.com>

Lewis, Sinclair. *Main Street and Babbitt*. New York: Library of America, 1992.

Lowell, Robert. <www.xenowave.com/quotes.htm>

Loyd, Anthony. *My War Gone By, I Miss It So*. New York: Penguin, 1999.

Lueders, Edward. *The Clam Lake Papers: A Winter in the North Woods*. Ellison Bay, WI: William Caxton, 1996.

Maclean, Norman. *A River Runs through It and Other Stories*. Chicago: University of Chicago Press, 2001.

Mailer, Norman. <www.famousquotesandauthors.com>

Marx, Groucho. <www.brainyquote.com>

McCarthy, Cormac. *Blood Meridian: Or the Evening Redness in the West*. New York: Vintage, 1992.

McConkey, James. *The Anatomy of Memory: An Anthology*. New York: Oxford, 1996.

McGuane, Thomas. *Some Horses: Essays*. New York: Vintage, 2000.

McNamara, Robert. *In Retrospect: The Tragedy and Lesson of Vietnam*. With Brian VanDeMark. New York: Random House, 1995.

Melville, Herman. *Moby-Dick*. New York: Norton Critical Edition, 1967.

Menand, Louis. <http://www.newyorker.com/arts/critics/>

Mendelsohn, Daniel. <http://www.newyorker.com/arts/critics/books/>

Merwin, W. S. *Migration: New & Selected Poems*. Port Townsend, WA: Copper Canyon, 2007.

Miller, Arthur. *Death of a Salesman*. New York: Penguin, 1996.

Milosz, Czeslaw. <http://www.nytimes.com/2009/09/27/books/review/White-t. html>

Mitchell, Joni. <http://artists.letssingit.com/ joni-mitchell-lyrics-big-yellow-taxi-tsgr9wh>

Mondrian, Piet. <realitybitesartblog.blogspot.com/2011_02_01_archive.html>

Momaday, N. Scott. *The Names: A Memoir*. Tucson: University of Arizona Press, 1987.

Montague, C. E. <www.thinkexist.com>

Morgan, Robert. *Good Measure: Essays, Interviews, and Notes on Poetry*. Baton Rouge: Louisiana State University Press, 1993.

———. "Nail Bag." In *At the Edge of the Orchard Country*. Middletown, CT: Wesleyan University Press, 1987.

———. "Spirit Level." In *Sigodlin*. Middletown, CT: Wesleyan University Press, 1990.

Morris, Wright. *Love among the Cannibals*. Lincoln: University of Nebraska Press, 1977.

Morrison, Toni. In *A Jury of Her Peers: American Women Writers from Anne Bradstreet to Annie Proulx*, edited by Elaine Showalter. London: Virago Press, 2010.

Nadelson, Theodore. *Trained to Kill: Soldiers at War*. Baltimore: Johns Hopkins University Press, 2005.

Newman, Barnett. <http://www.goodreads.com>

Newton, Peter, qtd. in *Haiku: A Poet's Guide*. By Lee Gurga. Lincoln, IL: Modern Haiku Press, 2003.

Nietzsche, Friedrich. <www.thinkexist.com>

Nixon, Richard Milhous. *Memoirs of Richard Nixon* Cutchogue, NY: Buccaneer Books, 1994.

Noir, Guy. <www.imdb.com/character/ch0017880/quotes>

O'Brien, Tim. *The Things They Carried*. New York: Broadway, 1990.

———. "The Vietnam in Me." *New York Times Book Review*, October 2, 1994.

O'Connor, Flannery. *The Habit of Being: Letters of Flannery O'Connor*. New York: Farrar, Straus and Giroux, 1988.

———. < www.goodreads.com>

O'Hara, Frank. <http://pbk.fsu.edu/Announcement/spring2009speech.html>

Olsen, Tillie. "Tell Me a Riddle." In *Tillie Olsen (Women Writers: Texts and Contexts)*, edited by Deborah Silverton Rosenfelt. Piscataway, NJ: Rutgers University Press, 1995.

Olson, James S., and Randy Roberts, eds. *My Lai: A Brief History with Documents*. New York: Palgrave Macmillan, 1998.

Ondaatje, Michael. *The English Patient.* New York: Vintage, 1992.

Petraeus, David. <www.newsweek.com/id/123475>

Piaget, Jean. Qtd. in "Memory," *The Skeptic's Dictionary,* edited by Robert Todd Carroll <http://skepdic.com/memory.html>

Pound, Ezra. <www.poets.org/viewmedia.php/prmMID/19705>

Power, Thomas "Tommy." <http://www.japanfocus.org/-mark-selden/2414>

Pritchett, V. S. *A Cab at the Door & Midnight Oil.* New York: Modern Library, 1994.

Rankin, Jeannette. <www.goodreads.com/quotes>

Reagan, Ronald. <www.brainyquote.com>

Ritterbusch, Dale. *Lessons Learned: Poetry of the Vietnam War and Its Aftermath.* Woodbridge, CT: Viet Nam Generations & Burning Cities Press, 1995.

Rogers, Thomas. *The Confession of a Child of the Century.* New York: Simon & Schuster, 1972.

Rose, Stephen. *The Making of Memory from Molecules to Mind.* New York: Doubleday, 1993.

Rosen, Jennifer. *Waiter, There's a Horse in My Wine.* Denver: Dauphin Press, 2005.

Rumsfeld, Donald. <http://www.slate.com/id/2081042/>

Sallah, Michael and Mitch Weiss. *Tiger Force: A True Story of Men and War.* New York: Back Bay, 2006.

Saner, Reg. *So This Is the Map.* New York: Random House, 1981.

Santayana, George. <www.quotationsbook.com>

Sante, Luc. *The Factory of Facts.* New York: Random House, 1998.

Schacter, Daniel L. *Searching for Memory: The Brain, the Mind, and the Past.* New York: Basic Books, 1996.

Service, Robert. *The Cremation of Sam McGee.* Toronto: Kids Can Press, 2006.

Shelley, Percy Bysshe. *Shelley's Poetry and Prose.* New York: Norton Critcal Edition, 2002.

Shields, David. *Reality Hunger: A Manifesto.* New York: Vintage, 2011.

Silko, Leslie Marmon. *Ceremony.* New York: Penguin, 2006.

Skinner, Jeffrey. *Gender Studies.* Miami: Miami University Press, 2002.

Sklarew, Myra. Heard in a public presentation, but see <www.poetrytherapy.org/pdf/NAPTmuseletter.200707.pdf>

Snyder, Gary. <http://poemhunter.blogspot.com/2008/04/after-weeks-of-watching-roof-leak.html>

Stafford, William. In *Some Haystacks Don't Even Have Any Needle, and Other Complete Modern Poems,* edited by Stephen Dunning, Edward G. Lueders, and Hugh Letcher Smith. New York: Scott Foresman, 1969.

Stanton, Doug. *Horse Soldiers: The Extraordinary Story of a Band of U.S. Soldiers Who Rode to Victory in Afghanistan.* New York: Scribner, 2009.

Strand, Mark. <www.poets.org>

Szymborska, Wislawa. *Poems New and Collected.* New York: Mariner, 2000.

215

Thomas, Lewis. *Lives of a Cell: Notes of a Biology Watcher.* New York: Penguin, 1978.

Trotsky, Leon. <http://www.goodreads.com>

Turner, Brian. *Here, Bullet.* Farmington, ME: Alice James Books, 2005.

Twain, Mark. <www.goodreads.com/quotes>

Twichell, Chase. *Horses Where the Answers Should Have Been: New and Selected Poems.* Port Townsend, WA: Copper Canyon, 2010.

Tyson, Mike. <www.brainyquote.com>

Ullman, Ellen. "Dining with Robots." In *The Best American Science & Nature Writing,* edited by Susan Orleans. New York: Mariner, 2005.

Updike, John. *Too Far to Go: The Maples Stories.* New York: Fawcett, 1982.

Urquhart, Robert. "Two Poems." Paris Review, 162: Summer 2002: 230–31.

Vegetius. <http://www.military-quotes.com/vetetius-renatus.htm>

Voltaire. <www.thinkexist.com>

Vonnegut, Kurt. <www.goodreads.com>

Waits, Tom. <http://edit.mp3lyrics.org/t/tom-waits/pony/>

Warren, Robert Penn. *The Collected Poems.* Edited by John Burt. Baton Rouge: Louisiana State University Press, 1998.

Weil, Simone. <www.brainyquote.com>

West, Paul. *The Secret Lives of Words.* New York: Harcourt, 2000.

Wilbur, Richard. *Collected Poems 1943–2004.* New York: Mariner, 2006.

Williams, C. K. *Love about Love.* Keene, NY: Ausable Press, 2001.

Williams, Tennessee. *A Streetcar Named Desire.* New York: New Directions, 2004.

Wilson, Robley, Jr. *Everything Paid For.* Gainesville: University Press of Florida, 1999.

Wolfe, Tom. *The Right Stuff.* New York: Picador, 2008.

Wolff, Tobias. "A Practicum." In *Sudden Fiction: American Short-Short Stories,* edited by Robert Shapard and James Thomas. Salt Lake City: Peregrine Smith, 1986.

———. *This Boy's Life: A Memoir.* New York: Grove Press, 1989.

Yeats, William Butler. <www.yeatsvision.com/Shelley.html>

Zimmer, Paul. *Crossing to Sunlight: Selected Poems.* Athens: University of Georgia Press, 1996.

Permissions